Zen Vibes

A Teen's Guide to Self-Discovery

John Lee, M.D.

Uri Collective

Illustrations and Editing by Damhee D. Hong

Acknowledgments: Portions of this work were created with the assistance of artificial intelligence technology.

With deep gratitude to the young people walking their own brave paths,
the families who hold space with love and patience,
and the clinicians who continue to show up with wisdom, presence, and care.

Your courage, compassion, and commitment are the threads that weave this work together.

This book wouldn't exist without you — and it's written with you in mind.

Contents

Welcome to Your Mind

You probably spend a lot of time in your head.
But how often do you actually look at your mind?

Most of us are taught how to study, how to work, how to hustle.

But we're rarely taught how to understand our thoughts, how to listen to our emotions, how to connect with our inner self, or how to feel okay just being who we are. We're also not often shown how to connect with something bigger, like a sense of meaning, presence, or our place in the world.

That's what this book is here to explore.

You could call it mindfulness. You could call it spirituality.
You could also just call it learning to work with both your inner world and the world around you in a way that actually makes sense.

This isn't about forcing yourself to "think positive" or pretending everything's fine when it isn't. It's about slowing down enough to hear yourself clearly, and building a kind of trust in who you are underneath all the pressure.

By the end of this book, you'll have tools to:

-Understand your thoughts without getting stuck in them
-Feel emotions without being overwhelmed by them
-Notice what truly matters to you
-Make space for your real self to show up
-See your life with more meaning, presence, and peace

This isn't a guide to becoming some perfect version of yourself.
It's an invitation to remember the self that's been here all along.

Let's start there.

Quote: "Smile, breathe, and go slowly." Thich Nhat Hanh
Song: "We Move Lightly" Dustin O'Halloran

Chapter One

Understanding Your Mental Landscape

Introduction: Understanding Your Inner World

Ever feel like your mind is a nonstop group chat, just you, overthinking everything? One minute you're focused, the next you're spiraling over something random from three years ago. The mental chatter, the self-doubt, the constant noise can feel exhausting.

But here's the thing: Overthinking and spirals are part of being human. That chatter isn't the real you. It's just your mind doing what minds do. When you learn to step back from it, something shifts. You begin to respond from a place that feels more grounded, more true, and more like yourself.

How Thoughts and Ego Shape Your Experience

Every day, your brain is like a night sky, scattered with thousands of thoughts like stars. Some thoughts are bright and creative. Others are heavy and anxious. Some shoot across the sky quickly, while others linger like distant galaxies. As we move through our day, these thoughts constantly appear, pulling our attention in different directions.

At the same time, there's another force at work in your mind: your ego. The ego is the voice inside that focuses on your identity, how you see yourself, and how others see you. It's the part that often asks, "Who am I?" and "How do I compare to others?"

This is where the ego starts connecting the dots. It draws constellations from your thoughts and turns them into stories about yourself.

"These stars prove I'm not good enough."
"Those ones show why I have to be the best."
"Here's the shape that says I don't belong."

To see how this works:
Thoughts are like stars—scattered, flickering, always moving.
Ego is the constellation—your mind trying to connect those stars into a story about who you are.
But you are the entire sky—the quiet, endless space that holds it all, without needing to chase or fix any of it.

Why This Matters

So why spend time looking at your thoughts and ego?

Because once you see how they're running the show, you stop being dragged around by them. You start to notice patterns, like how one self-doubting thought can snowball into a full-blown identity crisis. Or how your ego gets *real loud* right before you try something new.

And suddenly, you have something you didn't before.
Space. Space to pause. Space to decide what's real. Space to choose how you want to respond.

That's what this chapter is here to help you build:
More awareness
More freedom
A stronger connection to who you really are, beneath the noise

Let's dive into practical ways to recognize your thought patterns and discover the calm, clear sky of awareness that's been there all along.

1. Recognizing the Illusions of the Mind

You Are Not Your Mind

Let's start with Jess.

Whenever her friends didn't text back, she would spiral fast.
Her brain would say things like:

"Everyone hates me."
"I probably annoyed them."
"They're done with me."

It didn't feel like just a thought. It felt like the truth.
Like something had to be wrong with her.

But one day, mid-spiral, Jess caught herself.
She paused and thought,

"Wait... who's noticing this thought?"

She realized something huge. The thought wasn't her. It was just a habit. And she didn't have to believe it.

Now, when her mind starts spiraling, she still notices the thoughts.
But she doesn't panic. She doesn't sink.
She watches. She breathes. She stays steady.

The One Who Notices

Like Jess, you've probably had thoughts pop into your head that hit hard:

"I'm not good enough."
"Everyone thinks I'm weird."
"I'm going to fail."

In the moment, those thoughts feel real. They feel like facts.

But pause for a second.

If a thought pops into your head, and you can notice it... who's doing the noticing?

Really think about that.

If your brain is constantly throwing out thoughts, but there's a part of you that can step back and go,

"Whoa, where did that even come from?"

Then who's the real you?
You're not the thoughts.
You're the one watching the thoughts.

There's a quiet part of you that sees it all.
Not judging. Not overreacting. Just noticing.
And when you realize that's actually you, you get a different kind of freedom.

Your thoughts might still be loud.
They might still come in strong.
But now, you don't have to believe everything they say.

Choosing Which Thoughts to Believe

Jess still has anxious thoughts sometimes. That didn't stop.
But now, she questions them.

She knows:
Not every thought is the truth.
Some are just old patterns.
Some are protective habits her brain learned to keep her safe, but now they keep her stuck.

This is where it all begins. Simply by noticing.
Which brings us to a big one...

Mind Tricks: When Your Brain Plays Games

Ever get stuck in your head, replaying something over and over?
You overanalyze a DM. Worry about how you came across. Or obsess over what someone might be thinking about you.

And even though it's exhausting, part of your brain is like, "If I think about this just a little longer, I'll figure it out."

Spoiler: The more you overthink, the messier it gets… and the further you drift from what's actually real.

Overthinking = The Mental Version of Doom-Scrolling

Overthinking is kind of like scrolling on social media.
You start with one post…
Then you scroll, scroll, scroll…
And suddenly you've spent an hour spiraling through stuff that makes you anxious, jealous, or just plain drained.

It's hard to stop, right?

That's exactly how overthinking works.
One tiny thought turns into a full mental feed.
Each thought feeds the next.
Before you know it, you're stuck in a mind loop, and everything feels way more dramatic than it actually is.

And here's the wild part: **Your brain thinks it's helping you. But it's just keeping you stuck.**

The Impact of Overthinking

Overthinking doesn't just make life complicated. It actually messes with your brain.

Neuroscientists say it activates the same parts of the brain that deal with anxiety and stress. Your mind's alarm system goes off, even when there's no actual danger. The longer you overthink, the harder it is to feel calm or think clearly.

Let's say you wave at a friend across the street. They don't wave back.
No big deal, right?

Unless...

"Did they ignore me on purpose?"
"Are they mad at me?"
"What if they don't like me anymore?"

Now you're spiraling. Replaying every conversation. Questioning your worth. Overthinking turns a small moment into a full-blown rejection that never even happened.

The Comparison Trap

Just like social media, overthinking can trap you in comparison mode.

"Why didn't I get invited?"
"How are they doing so much better than me?"
"What if I'm falling behind?"

Your brain twists things around until everything feels worse than it actually is. And the longer you stay stuck in that loop, the harder it is to remember what's actually true.

The Freeze Mode: When Overthinking Stops You from Living

Ever try to post a photo or pick a caption... but second-guess yourself until you just give up?

That's freeze mode.
Overthinking creates stress.

It messes with your sleep.
It makes every decision feel like a huge deal.

And the more you do it, the more your brain thinks this is the way to stay "safe."

"If I just keep thinking, I'll figure it out."

But nope.
Overthinking doesn't lead to answers. It just creates more mental clutter.

Breaking the Cycle

Here's the good news: you can break the cycle.

Just like you can choose to stop scrolling, you can choose to hit pause on your mental feed. It starts with awareness, noticing when you've fallen into the trap.

Thinking vs. Awareness

There's a big difference between these two.
Thinking = that non stop inner voice—judging, doubting, narrating everything.
Awareness = the part of you that can step back, observe the noise, and go, "Whoa... I don't have to believe all of this."

Overthinking is just a trick your mind plays on you.
The real power comes when you stop falling for it.

Because when you stop living in your head... You start living in real life.

The Way Forward

You don't have to stay stuck in overthinking mode forever.

Just like you can put your phone down and step away from the scroll, you can do the same with your thoughts.

And it all starts with one simple shift.

Learning how to notice what your mind is doing, without getting pulled into every mental rabbit hole.

That's where this next tool comes in.

Mindful Noting: The First Step Toward Mental Clarity

Mindful Noting is a powerful practice that helps you step back from the noise instead of being consumed by it. Over time, it teaches you how to shift from **reacting** to **observing**, from spiraling to staying steady.

What *Is* Mindful Noting?

Mindful Noting is exactly what it sounds like: You *note* what's happening in your mind, without judging it.

Instead of getting pulled into thoughts like:

"I'm going to fail."
"They probably hate me."
"Why am I even thinking about this?"

You take a breath... and mentally label what's happening:

"That's a thought about failing."
"That's self-doubt showing up."
"That's me noticing my overthinking."

You're not trying to stop your thoughts. (That's impossible.) You're just *watching* them instead of becoming them.

How to Practice Mindful Noting IRL

Here's how you can apply Mindful Noting in everyday moments. Instead of getting pulled into spirals, you pause, name what's happening, and step into observer mode.

We'll revisit these situations later in the book, so don't worry about getting it perfect now. Just start noticing.

Social Situations

1. The Text Spiral (Left on Read)
Thought: "They're ignoring me."
Reaction: Anxiety. Insecurity.

Mindful Noting
"That's fear of being unwanted."
"That's nervous energy building up."
"That's me noticing my need for connection."

2. The Outfit Comment
Thought: "Do I look weird right now?"
Reaction: Embarrassment. Self-doubt.

Mindful Noting
"That's social anxiety showing up."
"That's my brain trying to keep me safe."
"That's me noticing my sensitivity to judgment."

3. You Worry You Said Something Weird
Thought: *"Did I sound weird just now?"*
Reaction: Embarrassment. Replay loop.

Mindful Noting
"That's social anxiety."
"That's my brain scanning for danger."
"That's me noticing my self-doubt."

Personal Moments

1. Waking Up in a Funk
Thought: No specific thought—just feeling off.
Reaction: Low energy. Disconnected.

Mindful Noting
"That's a mood drop."

"That's my body in a low state."
"That's me noticing the heaviness."

2. Snapping and Regretting It

Thought: *"Why did I say that?"*
Reaction: Guilt. Shame spiral.

Mindful Noting

"That's regret surfacing."
"That's my inner critic getting loud."
"That's me noticing how I'm treating myself."

3. Decision Paralysis

Thought: *"What if I choose the wrong thing?"*
Reaction: Stuck. Overwhelmed.

Mindful Noting

"That's fear of making mistakes."
"That's perfectionism showing up."
"That's me noticing my indecision."

School Situations

1. Bombing a Quiz

Thought: *"I knew I'd mess up."*
Reaction: Shame. Self-doubt.

Mindful Noting

"That's disappointment."
"That's me being hard on myself."
"That's me noticing my inner pressure."

2. Procrastinating

Thought: *"I'll start later..."*
Reaction: Avoidance. Background stress.

Mindful Noting

"That's resistance to discomfort."

"That's my brain seeking escape."
"That's me noticing the urge to delay."

3. Needing Help but Not Asking
Thought: *"They'll think I'm dumb."*
Reaction: Silence. Feeling stuck.

Mindful Noting
"That's fear of judgment."
"That's vulnerability I'm avoiding."
"That's me noticing my hesitation."

Family Situations

1. Parent Criticizes You
Thought: *"They never see what I do right."*
Reaction: Defensiveness. Hurt.

Mindful Noting
"That's frustration rising."
"That's old pain being triggered."
"That's me noticing my emotional response."

2. Worried About Their Reaction
Thought: *"They're going to freak out."*
Reaction: Tension. Hiding the truth.

Mindful Noting
"That's fear of conflict."
"That's anxiety in my chest."
"That's me noticing my self-protection kicking in."

3. Not Being Allowed to Go Out
Thought: *"They don't trust me."*
Reaction: Anger. Powerlessness.

Mindful Noting
"That's disappointment."

"That's me wanting freedom."
"That's me noticing my frustration."

You'll come back to these situations later in the book. You'll learn how to untangle them, respond differently, and rewire the patterns underneath. For now, just practice **noticing what's showing up.**

The goal isn't to eliminate thoughts or feelings. It's to notice them clearly so they don't take over your entire vibe.

Mindful Noting Practice

Pick a moment from today when you felt stressed, anxious, or overwhelmed. Use the space below to walk through it.

1. What happened?
(Briefly describe the situation)

2. What thought showed up?
"I thought..."

3. What did you feel in your body?
(Tight chest? Nausea? Restlessness?)

4. What was your reaction?
(What did you do or want to do?)

5. Now try Mindful Noting:

"That's ____."

"That's ____ showing up."

"That's me noticing ____."

Mindful Noting serves as the foundation upon which we'll build throughout this book. As you become more comfortable observing your thoughts rather than being consumed by them, you'll develop the mental clarity needed for the deeper practices ahead. This simple technique creates space between you and your reactions. Space that allows for choice rather than automatic response. Consider it your entry point into a more mindful relationship with your inner world. As we progress, this foundational skill will help you navigate the more nuanced aspects of self-awareness and emotional regulation we'll explore together.

2. The Fake ID: Meet Your Ego

So, you've started to notice your thoughts. The spirals. The fears. The random, dramatic self-talk.

But have you ever asked: **Where are these thoughts even coming from?**

Why do some of them sound so harsh? Why do they care so much about being liked, being right, being *something*? That voice. The one that compares you to everyone else. That panics when you're left out, or whispers *"You're only enough if..."* That voice?

That's your ego.

Imagine carrying around a fake ID, one that says you're someone you're really not. You use it so often, you start to believe it's actually you. That's what the ego does. It builds a version of you out of stories, roles, and rules, like:

- "I'm the chill one. I can't show how I really feel."

- "I'm the outsider. I'll never belong."

- "I'm the high achiever. If I fail, I'm nothing."

- "I'm the victim. People always hurt me."

It doesn't matter whether the story is about being *the best* or *the one who's always left behind*, the ego just wants something to latch onto. Something that helps you feel safe, seen, or in control.

But here's the truth: **Your ego is not the real you.** It's just a mask, one your mind builds to protect you, win approval, or avoid pain.

The *real* you? It's that quiet awareness underneath all of it. The part of you that can pause, look at the mask, and ask:

"Do I actually have to keep being this version of me?"

Once you learn how to spot the ego's tricks, you start to get your power back.

How Your Ego Runs the Show

Here's how your ego shows up.

It craves validation. It wants likes, compliments, approval. It wants proof that you're *good enough*.

It freaks out when things go wrong. One mistake? The ego sees it as *failure*. Not being picked? The ego says *you're not wanted*.

It gets defensive. If someone calls you out or disagrees? The ego jumps in to protect its story because it thinks being wrong means being unworthy.

It plays roles. The smart one. The funny one. The outcast. The fixer. Whatever identity helped you feel seen or safe, your ego clings to it.

It builds identity out of external stuff.

What other people think.

How much attention you get.

How much control you feel.

Whether you're winning, liked, admired, or "right."

And sometimes? Even pain becomes part of the ego's identity.

If being the one who's always left out or misunderstood gave you something to hold onto, your ego might protect *that* just as fiercely as it would any praise.

This happens a lot, especially during the teen years. Think about it. If you've spent years as "the friend no one remembers to invite," or "the one whose opinions get ignored," that painful label starts feeling like part of who you are. It's messed up, but sometimes there's comfort in a label that hurts because at least it's familiar.

Your brain gets really good at collecting evidence that proves your painful story is true. When someone leaves you on read, when you're not included in the group chat, when no one comments on your post, your brain jumps to: "See? This is exactly what always happens to me." And in a weird way, being right about how you'll be treated feels better than being wrong, even if it means staying stuck in pain.

What makes this super complicated is that maybe some of this really did happen to you. Maybe people actually did overlook you or make you feel less important. That doesn't mean it has to define your future, though. The tricky part is that when you've carried around a painful identity for years, the thought of letting it go feels scary. Without it, who would you even be? What would explain why things happen the way they do?

Breaking this pattern takes real courage because you're basically saying goodbye to a version of yourself you've known forever. It means being willing to see yourself differently, even when your mind keeps trying to drag you back to the familiar pain. That's why just "thinking positive" rarely works on its own. You're not just changing your thoughts, you're challenging a whole identity you've built.

The Hidden Cost

Living through the ego is **exhausting**. You're always chasing something like approval, control, proof that you matter, and avoiding anything that might make you feel rejected, embarrassed, or small.

It pulls you away from your actual self, the one who doesn't need to perform, defend, or impress.

We're not here to fight the ego. We're here to notice it. To loosen its grip. To start living from the part of you that's real, not the part that's always trying to be enough.

The Many Faces of Ego: Stories We Tell Ourselves

Let's meet a few people and their ego-stories. (Some of these might feel familiar.)

Cam's Story: The "Funny Guy" Pressure

Cam is the funny one. The class clown. The go-to person when things get awkward. Laughter is how he connects, how he gets seen, and how he feels safe.

But then someone new joins the group. Just as funny. Maybe even funnier.

Cam feels himself shift. Suddenly, he's not joking for fun anymore. He's performing to prove something. He interrupts, one-ups, and tries to stay on top of every punchline. If people laugh louder at someone else, his stomach tightens.

His ego whispers: "If I'm not the funniest, I don't matter."

He starts measuring his worth by the reaction he gets. Every moment becomes a performance. Every silence feels like failure. And slowly, the thing that used to bring him joy becomes exhausting.

He wonders what it would feel like to just be...himself.

Lena's Story: Performing to Belong

Lena never cared about indie music. Then her crush mentioned their favorite band, and everything changed.

She memorizes lyrics, follows the band, and posts about them like she's always been a fan.

Not out of love for the music, but because her ego sees a chance: "If I seem cool to them, they'll like me. And if they like me, I'll matter."

Lena starts shaping her voice, her style, her personality around who she thinks she needs to be. At first, it feels exciting. Like she's stepping into a better version of herself. But over time, it gets harder to tell where her act ends and she begins. She laughs at jokes she doesn't find funny. Pretends to know references she's never heard. And slowly, the space between her and her real self grows wider.

Her ego promises belonging, but it comes at the cost of authenticity.

Maya's Story: The "Strong One" Mask

Maya grew up hearing the same messages again and again: "Be strong." "Don't complain." "Push through."

Now, even when she's overwhelmed, she says she's fine. Even when she wants to cry, she smiles.

Her ego says, "If I fall apart, I'll be a burden. And if I'm a burden, I won't be loved."

So she stays quiet. She handles everything on her own. She becomes the one people rely on, even when she's running on empty. But the more she hides her struggle, the more isolated she feels. And the more she pretends she's okay, the harder it becomes to ask for help.

Her ego tells her she's strong for keeping it all in. But the truth is, it takes more strength to be seen.

Zara's Story: The Outcast Armor

Zara knows what it feels like to be left out. To not be chosen. To feel invisible in a room full of people.

So now, she leans into it. She says she doesn't care. She calls people fake. NPCs. She tells herself she's better off alone.

But it's not confidence. It's armor.

Her ego says, "If you don't try to belong, you can't be rejected."

So she rejects others first. She wears her difference like a badge. Like proof that she doesn't need anyone. But deep down, she does. She wants connection. She wants closeness. She just doesn't know how to want those things without fear.

The outcast identity protects her, but it also isolates her. And behind the armor, there's still a heart hoping to be let in.

Aiden's Story: Perfection or Nothing

Aiden has always been the smart one. The overachiever. The kid who gets everything right. But one bad grade? One mistake? And suddenly, his chest tightens. His thoughts spiral.

His ego starts talking fast: "You're slipping. You have to fix this. If you're not perfect, who are you?"

He studies harder. Sleeps less. Pushes past his limits. On the outside, he still looks like he has it all together.

But inside? He's anxious. Exhausted. Trapped.

His ego builds his worth on success, but never lets him rest. Because every win resets the pressure. And every stumble feels like proof that he's not enough.

He wonders what it might feel like to just be human.

Talia's Story: The Need to Be Right

Talia loves deep conversations. She's curious, reflective, and likes to think things through. But when someone disagrees with her, she can feel tense. Her words get sharper. Her patience gets shorter. Her ego says, "If you're wrong, you're weak. If they win, you lose."

So she pushes back. She talks over. She dismisses. Even when part of her wants to listen, another part shuts the door.

Talia doesn't mean to come off cold. But for her ego, being right feels like protection. Like proof that she matters.

Later, she replays the moment and feels the discomfort. Not because she lost the argument—but because she missed the chance to connect.

Jonah's Story: Holding Onto the Sadness

Jonah feels everything deeply. He always has. At some point, his sadness stopped being a feeling—and started becoming part of his identity. He posts sad quotes. Calls himself "the broken one." Builds his aesthetic around being misunderstood.

And part of him wants to feel better. To move forward. But another part of him—his ego—whispers: "If I let go of this pain... who even am I?"

So Jonah stays stuck. Not because he likes being sad, but because sadness has become familiar. Safe. His ego tells him that healing might mean losing himself.

But it's not true. Healing doesn't erase who you are—it reveals the parts of you that got buried beneath the pain.

Nico's Story: The One Who Has It All Together

Nico grew up being the "responsible one." The one who doesn't mess up. The one who keeps everyone else calm. His family leans on him. Teachers praise him. Friends expect him to be the rock.

So he plays the part: always helpful, always composed, always fine. Even when he's not.

"If I fall apart, everything else will too." "I can't let people see me struggle." "I have to keep it together."

That's the story Nico's ego tells him. That his worth comes from being dependable. Unshakeable. Emotionally bulletproof.

But inside? He's exhausted. Carrying the pressure to be perfect—not just for himself, but for everyone around him. And he's terrified that if he lets go of that role... he won't know who he is without it.

These are just a few of the masks the ego learns to wear.

Some are loud and easy to spot. Others are quiet, shaped by years of little moments and invisible pressures. Everyone has their own version. Some people wear one mask all the time. Others shift depending on where they are or who they're with.

None of them are random. Each one forms around a need to feel something essential.

The ego isn't just chasing attention.

It's trying to feel:
Safe

Loved

Respected

Seen

In control

To meet those needs, it builds an identity:
The funny one
The cool one
The strong one
The outsider
The perfect one
The one who's always right
The broken one
The one who holds it all together

And a thousand other roles we try on just to feel okay.

The ego tells you this is who you have to be. That if you step out of the role, everything might fall apart.

But behind every mask, there is a part of you that never changed. The part that notices. The part that sees the performance and still remembers who you are underneath it all.

You don't need to erase the ego. You just need to notice it.

You can pause when it starts speaking.
You can soften when it tightens.
You can choose honesty instead of habit.

Connection instead of control.
Presence instead of performance.

Coming up next: how to recognize when your ego is leading and how to gently return to the version of you that doesn't need to perform to be real.

Name Your Ego: Calling It Out With Humor and Clarity

By now, you've seen it. Your ego isn't who you are.

It's just a voice that tries to protect you, impress others, or keep you from feeling exposed.

And one of the best ways to respond?
Give it a name.

Naming your ego helps you recognize when it shows up.
It gives you space to pause.
It reminds you that this voice is not your truth.

Give It a Nickname

Pick something that makes you smile or something that helps you spot it quickly.
Your nickname might reflect how your ego acts, how it speaks, or what it wants most.

Here are some ideas.

Panic Mode – spirals fast, assumes the worst

The Measurer – compares you to everyone else

Captain Cool – needs to impress and be liked

Doom Radio – plays dramatic, hopeless thoughts

The Fixer – wants total control and zero mistakes

Shadow Voice – brings up old shame or fear

The Narrator – creates stories that sound real but are just worry

You might call it "Static," "Bossy Brain," "Auto-Pilot," or anything that helps you recognize it quickly.

When you say to yourself, *"That sounds like Doom Radio again,"* you're no longer caught inside the story. You're present. You're observing. You're beginning to take charge.

Spotting Your Ego in Real Time

Imagine you get left out of a group hang.

Your ego might say:

"They don't really like you."
"You're always the one who gets left out."
"You should just stop trying."

This is a moment to pause.
You can take a breath.
You can notice what's happening and say, *"Panic Mode is loud today."*

Now you are not reacting. You are watching.
And when you're watching, you have choices.

Try This

When you feel nervous, upset, or on edge, ask yourself:

Who is speaking right now—me, or my ego?
What is this voice trying to protect?
Is this voice helping me grow or holding me back?

Asking questions like these helps you return to your awareness.
It reminds you that you are the one who chooses how to respond.

You Are Not the Ego

Your ego learned how to keep you safe a long time ago. It built roles. It created stories.
It wanted to help you feel important, accepted, and in control. These stories might
have worked before.

But you're growing now. You can notice the ego without following its lead.

You are already enough.
You do not need to be perfect.

You do not need to be impressive.
You do not need to prove anything to deserve love or belonging.

The next time the voice of the ego shows up, meet it with kindness.
Say, *"I see you. I hear you. But I'm choosing something different."*

The part of you that notices is the part that is steady and strong.
This is who you are. And this is the part you can return to anytime.

Chapter 1 Wrap-Up: More Than the Noise

Here's what we've explored so far.

Thoughts are not facts. They come and go like the weather.
The ego is not your true self. It's a story your mind created to help you feel safe.
The part of you that can notice all of this—that's your awareness. That's the real you.

When you begin to step back and observe your mind, it begins to loosen its grip.
And in that space, something quiet begins to show up.

Sometimes, beneath the thoughts, there is something deeper.
A heaviness. A sadness. A loneliness that lingers.
An ache you might not always know how to name.

That's what we're going to explore next.

In Chapter 2, we'll begin talking about emotional pain.
Not to stay in it, but to understand it. Because when you allow yourself to feel without being overwhelmed, healing begins. And healing makes space for something new to grow.

Quote: "I am not what happened to me, I am what I choose to become." Carl Jung
Song: "Heavy" Birdtalker

Chapter Two

Understanding Emotional Pain

Introduction

You've probably felt it before. That gut-drop moment when you realize you weren't invited. Or the quiet sting after an argument that keeps looping in your head days later.

Emotional pain doesn't fade the way physical pain sometimes does. You can't just ice it and move on. It tends to linger. It loops through your thoughts. It sticks around longer than expected. Sometimes for weeks, months, or even years. Like a memory you didn't mean to hold, but still carry with you. And just like physical pain tells you to check in with your body, emotional pain asks you to check in with your heart. To listen. To respond.

But before we can talk about how to heal, we need to understand what an emotion really is.

Emotions are messengers. Not instructions. Not facts. Not flaws.

They carry signals. They show up to reflect something happening inside you. Maybe it's a need, a boundary, a fear, or a desire.

Think of emotions like letters from yourself, sent straight from your inner world. Each one is telling you something important about what's going on beneath the surface. But sometimes we treat those letters like spam. We either ignore them completely or act on them instantly, without even reading what they say.

Imagine if you treated your actual spam mail the way we sometimes treat emotions. You get a message that says, "You've won a million dollars! But first, send us all your money." And instead of stopping to think, you're like, "Okay!!" It's like running away the second you feel the first bit of panic, without even checking what it's really about.

Not every emotion needs an emergency reaction. Most of them deserve to be opened, read, and understood.

The key is to pause and check. What is this emotion trying to say? Is it asking for care? Is it pointing to something that matters?

Emotions aren't here to control you. They're here to guide you. The more you learn to read the message, the less it runs the show.

And that brings us to an important concept.

When we're babies, we don't hold back. If we're scared, we cry. If we're hungry, we scream. If we're curious, we reach. We react right away. That's how we survive.

As we grow, our brain is supposed to build new tools. We start learning how to pause. To notice what we're feeling. To name it. To express it in ways that help us feel safe, connected, and understood.

That's **emotional development.**

Some reactions still need to be quick. Like if you see a bear, you don't journal about it. You run. That's instinct. But not everything in life is a bear. Not every uncomfortable feeling needs an emergency response.

Emotional growth is learning to tell the difference. It's learning when to slow down, so you're not treating every challenge like danger.

But sometimes that growth gets interrupted.

If you were taught to stay quiet.
If you were shamed for crying or told you were too sensitive.
If you had to be the one who kept it together.

You might have learned to hide what you felt just to get by. To act tough. To stay small. To pretend things didn't bother you, even when they did.

And if you lived in survival mode for a long time, your brain may not have had the chance to develop those emotional tools. It stayed focused on protection, not reflection.

So instead of learning how to work with your emotions, you kept reacting like everything was a threat. You shut down. You snapped. You smiled when you were hurting. Not because you're broken, but because your brain did what it thought it had to do.

Now, you get to try something different. You get to learn what your emotions are actually trying to say, and how to respond in ways that feel safe and true to you.

You don't have to stay stuck in old patterns. You're allowed to grow. You're allowed to feel. You're allowed to heal.

This isn't about ignoring your feelings or pretending things are okay when they aren't. It's about learning how to be with those feelings in a way that feels steady, kind, and safe.

It's about recognizing what your emotions are trying to tell you and giving yourself the space to really listen.

Here's what we'll explore together:

- What emotional pain really feels like and why it often sticks around

- How fear, avoidance, and overthinking add extra weight

- The link between emotional pain and your mental well-being

- Tools like journaling, self-compassion, and visualization to help you move through discomfort without shutting down

By the end of this chapter, you'll have more clarity and support to meet your emotions with understanding. You may begin to see emotional pain not as a sign that something's wrong, but as a sign that something is ready to be seen, felt, and cared for.

1. The Nature of Emotional Pain

Emotional pain weaves itself into how you think, how you cope, and how you connect. It shapes what you expect from yourself and from others, even when you're not fully aware of it.

You might be laughing with friends, and suddenly feel out of place. You get a compliment, and something inside you questions it. You mess up something small, and your inner critic steps in fast.

That's emotional pain still moving underneath everything else.

Like when:

- A breakup from years ago still makes it hard to let people in

- A middle school moment still keeps you quiet in class

- Old teasing or bullying makes every joke feel personal

- A parent's voice still plays in your head when you mess up

- A friend's betrayal makes you question people who care about you

- Being compared to someone else makes you feel like you'll never be enough

- One big failure makes you freeze every time you want to try something new

You might think, "It's just a memory," but emotional pain doesn't always stay in the past. It can show up in how you respond to conflict, how close you let people get, and how you treat yourself when you fall short.

Even when the original moment is long gone, the impact can still be present in small ways. It weaves into your habits, your self-talk, and your expectations.

You might not remember the exact moment something hurt you, but your body remembers. So do your thoughts and reactions.

Over time, it starts to settle in.

It adds weight to the everyday.

And the longer you carry it, the heavier it gets.

The Emotional Backpack: Why Pain Stacks Up Over Time

Ever wonder why something small can hit so hard?

Like someone forgetting to text back feels like total rejection. Or a bad grade suddenly makes you feel like a failure in life. That's because you're not just reacting to that one thing, you're reacting to everything else you've been carrying.

Every time something hurtful happens, like a fight with a friend, being ghosted or feeling invisible or misunderstood, it adds something new to your *emotional backpack.*

And if you never unpack it? That weight starts affecting how you move through the world. The emotional backpack doesn't just make life heavier. It makes everything feel more overwhelming than it actually is.

But just like you take care of your body when it's hurt, you can take care of your emotions too. You can unpack the backpack. And you can learn how to feel pain without letting it run your life.

How Your Emotional Backpack Messes with You

Your emotional backpack doesn't just sit there. It changes how you react to things now.

You've been ghosted before → Now, if someone takes too long to reply, your brain goes *Here we go again*, and suddenly, you're spiraling.

You had a friend betray you → Now, every time someone cancels plans, it feels like they're pulling away—even if they're just busy.

You were embarrassed speaking in public → Now, raising your hand in class makes your stomach drop, even though no one remembers what happened last time.

And Here's the Shift: Emotional Pain Needs to Be Processed

Every time something painful happens and you don't have space to deal with it, you toss it into your emotional backpack and zip it up.

At first, it doesn't feel like much. Just a little weight. But over time, that backpack gets heavier. You start carrying it everywhere—through school, friendships, family stuff, even in quiet moments alone.

Unprocessed pain doesn't go away. It follows you.
It shows up when you shut down during a simple convo.
It slips out when you snap at someone who didn't actually do anything wrong.

You start asking:

"Why am I like this?"
"Why does this still bother me?"
"I thought I got over this..."

But the truth is:

You're not "too much."
You've just been carrying a lot without ever getting to unpack it.

Processing emotional pain is like taking off the backpack, opening it up, and actually looking at what's inside. You name what hurt. You feel it. You start to understand it. And little by little, that weight gets lighter. The first step? Noticing what's in there.

Because once you see what you've been holding onto, you can finally start letting it go. Let's start unpacking.

2. The Pain Monster: When Thoughts Keep Emotions Stuck

There's a name for what builds up when emotional weight isn't unpacked. We call it the **Pain Monster**.

It lives in the emotional backpack you carry. The one filled with unspoken fears, quiet sadness, self-doubt, and things you didn't get to express. When those feelings stay packed away, the Pain Monster starts to grow.

It feeds on the thoughts that loop. It grows when you judge yourself, when you hold things in, or when you try to ignore what's still bothering you.

It doesn't shout. It just adds weight.

Let's revisit some of the everyday moments from Chapter 1. This time through the lens of the Pain Monster, to see how unprocessed emotions quietly take over.

The Text Spiral

You send a text. It's been hours. Still no reply.

Your thoughts start spiraling:
"They're ignoring me."
"They're mad at me."
"I'm too much."

Now emotions kick in:
Anxiety.
Insecurity.
Loneliness.

And those emotions start giving orders:
"Keep checking your phone."
"Read the message over and over."
"Don't text again—you'll seem desperate."

The Pain Monster feeds on all that silence, turning a normal delay into a personal rejection.

The Outfit Comment

Someone says something shady about your outfit. You laugh it off, but it sticks.

Your thoughts start piling up:
"Do I look weird?"
"Why did I even wear this?"
"I should've played it safe."

Now emotions rush in:
Embarrassment.
Self-doubt.
Shame.

And the instructions follow:
"Change into something else."
"Delete that photo you posted."
"Don't try anything bold again."

The Pain Monster latches onto the moment, using one comment to shrink your confidence.

You Worry You Said Something Weird

You walk away from a conversation and can't stop replaying it.

Thoughts pile up fast:
"Did I sound weird just now?"
"They probably think I'm awkward."
"Why can't I act normal?"

Now you feel:
Embarrassed.
On edge.
Self-conscious.

The emotions push you to:
"Hide."

"Avoid talking next time."
"Rehearse everything before speaking."

The Pain Monster locks you in a loop, feeding off social anxiety and self-doubt.

Waking Up in a Funk

You wake up and instantly feel low, like something's off, but there's no clear reason.

Your brain starts wondering:
"Why do I feel like this?"
"Is something wrong with me?"
"I don't want to deal with today."

Emotions roll in heavy:
Low energy.
Disconnected.
Down for no reason.

And your mind suggests:
"Cancel everything."
"Don't talk to anyone."
"Just scroll and zone out."

The Pain Monster grows in silence, fed by the weight you haven't named.

Snapping and Regretting It

You say something in the heat of the moment. It wasn't kind.

The thoughts hit hard afterward:
"Why did I say that?"
"I'm the worst."
"I ruin everything."

The emotional wave follows:
Guilt.
Shame.
Regret.

The response is to:

"Avoid the person."

"Replay what happened again and again."

"Keep beating yourself up."

The Pain Monster uses that regret to hold you hostage inside your own head.

Decision Paralysis

You need to make a choice, but every option feels risky.

Thoughts pile up:

"What if I choose wrong?"

"I'll regret it either way."

"I don't trust myself."

Now you feel:

Frozen.

Overwhelmed.

Trapped in indecision.

And your brain tells you:

"Avoid it a little longer."

"Ask ten people for their opinion."

"Wait until it magically feels easier."

The Pain Monster thrives when you're stuck, turning fear into self-doubt.

Bombing a Quiz

You walk out of class knowing you didn't do well.

Thoughts slam in:

"I knew I'd mess up."

"I'm not smart enough."

"Everyone else probably did fine."

You feel:

Disappointed.

Embarrassed.
Full of self-doubt.

And the instructions start:
"Don't check your grade."
"Don't tell anyone."
"Pretend you don't care."

The Pain Monster builds out of the pressure, making one quiz feel like a reflection of your entire worth.

Procrastinating

You know what you need to do. But you keep putting it off.

Thoughts begin circling:
"I'll just start later…"
"What if I mess it up anyway?"
"I don't feel ready."

And now you're sitting with:
Avoidance.
Stress.
Background guilt.

The mind suggests:
"Watch something first."
"Organize your desk again."
"Tell yourself you'll start after one more break."

The Pain Monster takes all that avoidance and turns it into pressure you carry all day.

Needing Help but Not Asking

You're stuck, but asking for help feels terrifying.

Thoughts swirl:
"They'll think I'm dumb."

"I should already know this."
"What if they laugh?"

You feel:
Small.
Embarrassed.
Stuck and unsure.

So you respond:
"Say nothing."
"Keep pretending you're fine."
"Stay stuck instead of reaching out."

The Pain Monster grows every time you stay silent instead of asking for support.

Parent Criticizes You

You hear another comment about what you're doing wrong.

The thoughts jump in:
"They never see what I do right."
"I'll never be enough."
"Why do I even try?"

Now emotions stir up:
Defensiveness.
Hurt.
Emotional walls.

And you react by:
"Shutting down."
"Snapping back."
"Tuning them out completely."

The Pain Monster gathers every old criticism and layers it onto this one moment.

Worried About Their Reaction

You're afraid to tell your parents something. Maybe it's important, but you're bracing for a blow-up.

Thoughts race ahead:
"They're going to freak out."
"They won't understand."
"I'm going to get in trouble."

Emotions build fast:
Tension.
Fear.
Guilt before it even happens.

Your instincts say:
"Hide it."
"Lie if you have to."
"Keep everything to yourself."

The Pain Monster grows in secrets and stress.

Not Being Allowed to Go Out

You ask to go somewhere, and the answer's no.

Your brain immediately fires off:
"They don't trust me."
"They just want to control everything."
"I can't breathe in this house."

Now you feel:
Angry.
Powerless.
Frustrated.

And your next moves:
"Slam the door."

"Say something you'll regret."

"Shut down and disconnect."

The Pain Monster feeds on that stuck, explosive feeling where you just want to escape everything.

These examples show how emotional pain doesn't always look dramatic or obvious. It can hide in your habits, your reactions, your silence. The Pain Monster doesn't always announce itself. It creeps in through the little moments you brush off. These everyday spirals, shutdowns, and patterns aren't random. Once you learn to recognize the Pain Monster's presence, you can start meeting it with awareness instead of avoiding it or letting it take over.

How to Stop Feeding It

You don't have to keep feeding your Pain Monster. Every time you catch yourself spiraling, you have a choice:

Keep looping the painful thought.

Or pause and work through your emotions step by step.

This is where our **6-step Emotion Process** comes in. A practical method to stop feeding your Pain Monster and start reclaiming your power.

When you notice those familiar thought patterns taking over, instead of getting caught in the spiral, you'll learn how to name what's happening, create space around it, and respond in a way that serves you better.

You're allowed to feel hurt, sad, anxious, or left out. **But you don't have to build a home in that feeling.**

With the process we're about to explore, you can acknowledge your emotions without letting them define you. And every time you practice these steps? Your Pain Monster shrinks. And you get a little bit more of your power back.

Your Emotional Reset: The 6-Step Process

In Chapter 1, we talked about Mindful Noting—how to catch thoughts before they spiral? Well, this process is like the next level.

This is your go-to process for handling tough feelings, whether it's a moment of sadness, anxiety, disappointment, or just feeling "off." You don't have to ignore it. You tend to it. And here's how.

The 6 Steps to Emotional Clarity

1. Acknowledge: Name What You Feel

"What am I feeling right now?"

Just saying it out loud or in your head starts to take the edge off. You're not fixing it yet, just noticing.

Examples:

- "I feel anxious."

- "I feel hurt."

- "I feel overwhelmed."

2. Accept: Let It Be Without Judgment

"This is hard, but it's okay that I feel this way."

You're not being dramatic. You're being human. Instead of fighting the feeling, you breathe into it.

Examples:

- "It makes sense I'm upset. This matters to me."

- "This sadness feels heavy, but it's a valid response to what just happened."

3. Understand: Find the Deeper Need

"What is this emotion trying to tell me?"

Every emotion is a messenger. It's trying to point to a need that's not being met. This is your moment to listen.

Examples:

- Feeling anxious? You might need safety or reassurance.

- Feeling angry? You might need space or clearer boundaries.

- Feeling lonely? You might need connection or support.

4. De-identify: Separate the Story From the Truth

"This is something I'm feeling. It's not who I am." "What's the fact here? What's just my brain's interpretation?"

This is where you take your power back. You unhook yourself from the spiraling storyline.

Examples:

- Fact: "They canceled plans." Story: "No one wants to hang out with me."

- Fact: "I didn't get a text back." Story: "I'm annoying and too much."

See the difference? One grounds you. The other drags you under.

5. Express: Do Something That Moves the Feeling Through

"What's one thing I can do right now to care for this emotion?"

This is where action comes in. Not to fix it, but to let it move.

Examples:

- Feeling lonely? Reach out to someone, even just with a meme or check-in.

- Feeling overwhelmed? Go outside, write it out, or set a small boundary.

- Feeling angry? Move your body, take space, or say what you need calmly.

6. Integrate: Learn From the Emotion (So You Don't Just Repeat It)

"What did I learn from this?" "How can this help me grow?"

This isn't about silver linings. It's about insight. You're asking what this emotion revealed about your values, patterns, or deeper needs.

Examples:

- "This showed me I care more about feeling included than I admit."

- "I keep getting overwhelmed when I say yes to things I don't want."

- "I avoid conflict, and then it builds. Maybe I need to speak up sooner."

Why This Works

It gives your emotions space to breathe.

It helps you stay curious, not judgmental.

It separates feelings from identity.

It reminds you that you're the observer. Not the emotion itself.

This isn't about avoiding emotions. It's about working with them so they don't run the show.

Let's walk through a few real-life examples so you can see exactly how this process works when you're spiraling or overwhelmed.

Real-Life Emotional Reset: Using the 6 Steps When Emotions Hit

The Text Spiral (Left on Read)

What Your Brain Does: You send a text. No response.

"They're ignoring me."

"They're mad at me."

"I'm too much."

6 Steps

1. Acknowledge: "I feel anxious and unsure."

2. Accept: "It's normal to want a response when I reach out."

3. Understand: "This is a need for connection and reassurance."

4. De-identify: "Not getting a reply doesn't mean I'm unlovable."

5. Express: Give myself the connection I need by reaching out to someone else or doing something that grounds me in the moment.

6. Integrate: "My worth isn't tied to how quickly someone responds."

The Outfit Comment

What Your Brain Does: Someone says something shady about your outfit.

"Do I look weird?"

"Why did I wear this?"

"I shouldn't have tried."

6 Steps

1. Acknowledge: "That hurt. I feel self-conscious."

2. Accept: "I wanted to feel good today, so this stung more."

3. Understand: "This is showing a need to feel accepted and confident."

4. De-identify: "One comment doesn't define how I look or who I am."

5. Express: Remind myself why I wore it. Stand tall. Talk to a friend who hypes me up.

6. Integrate: "I'm allowed to take up space with my style, even if not everyone gets it."

You Worry You Said Something Weird

What Your Brain Does: You walk away from a convo and immediately start spiraling.

"Did I sound weird just now?"

"They probably think I'm awkward."

"I always say the wrong thing."

6 Steps

1. Acknowledge: "I'm feeling embarrassed and unsure."

2. Accept: "It makes sense—social moments can feel intense sometimes."

3. Understand: "This is social anxiety showing up, trying to protect me from judgment."

4. De-identify: "Feeling awkward doesn't mean I *am* awkward."

5. Express: Take a breath. Move your body. Talk it out with someone who gets it.

6. Integrate: "Next time I feel this way, I can remember that most people aren't replaying it like I am."

Waking Up in a Funk

What Your Brain Does: You feel off before the day even begins.

"What's wrong with me?"

"I should feel better."

"I don't have energy for anything."

6 Steps

1. Acknowledge: "I feel low and disconnected."

2. Accept: "Some days just start heavy."

3. Understand: "This might be pointing to emotional or physical fatigue."

4. De-identify: "This mood isn't who I am. It's just what I'm feeling."

5. Express: Give myself rest or gentle movement. Take one small action to support myself.

6. Integrate: "Low-energy days don't erase my progress—I can take care of myself through them."

Snapping and Regretting It

What Your Brain Does: You say something in anger and instantly regret it.

"Why did I do that?"

"I always ruin things."

"They'll never forgive me."

6 Steps

1. Acknowledge: "I'm feeling guilt and embarrassment."

2. Accept: "I acted from a reactive place. That happens."

3. Understand: "This is showing a need to feel in control and safe in relationships."

4. De-identify: "A mistake doesn't define who I am."

5. Express: Take ownership. Apologize if needed. Journal or talk about what set me off.

6. Integrate: "I can learn from this without shaming myself."

Decision Paralysis

What Your Brain Does: You're stuck between options.

"What if I mess up?"

"I don't trust myself."

"It'll all go wrong anyway."

6 Steps

1. Acknowledge: "I feel frozen and overwhelmed."

2. Accept: "It makes sense—this feels important."

3. Understand: "This shows a need for safety and clarity."

4. De-identify: "Indecision doesn't mean I'm incapable."

5. Express: "I'm going to break this down into smaller, safer steps. Instead of choosing everything at once, I'll pick one piece to explore or research more. I can ask someone I trust to help me think it through."

6. Integrate: "I don't need perfect choices to move forward—I just need momentum."

Bombing a Quiz

What Your Brain Does: You get a bad grade and spiral.
"I'm not smart enough."
"I'm falling behind."
"Why even try?"

6 Steps

1. Acknowledge: "I'm disappointed and frustrated."

2. Accept: "School matters to me—this stings."

3. Understand: "This touches on my need for competence and progress."

4. De-identify: "One quiz doesn't define my intelligence."

5. Express: Choose one small thing to review or get help with. Take a step toward clarity.

6. Integrate: "I can care about doing well without letting grades define me."

Procrastination Spiral

What Your Brain Does: You avoid the task, but it haunts you.
"I'll do it later."
"I always mess around."
"I'm falling behind."

6 Steps

1. Acknowledge: "I'm avoiding something uncomfortable."

2. Accept: "Avoidance is my brain trying to protect me from stress."

3. Understand: "This might be showing fear of failure or burnout."

4. De-identify: "Struggling to start doesn't mean I'm lazy."

5. Express: Set a 5-minute timer. Start with one thing.

6. Integrate: "Tiny actions still move me forward—and I can build from there."

Needing Help but Not Asking

What Your Brain Does: You're stuck, but afraid to raise your hand.
"They'll think I'm dumb."
"I should already know this."
"Everyone else is doing fine."

6 Steps

1. Acknowledge: "I feel anxious and embarrassed."

2. Accept: "It's hard to be vulnerable—I get it."

3. Understand: "This is showing a need for support and safety."

4. De-identify: "Asking for help doesn't make me weak—it shows courage."

5. Express: Reach out. Send a message or ask someone kind. Give yourself permission to receive support.

6. Integrate: "Support exists—and I'm allowed to ask for it."

Parent Criticizes You

What Your Brain Does: Another comment lands like a punch.

"They never see what I do right."

"I'm not enough."

"Why do I even try?"

6 Steps

1. Acknowledge: "I feel angry and hurt."

2. Accept: "Their words impacted me—it's okay to feel this way."

3. Understand: "This is showing a need to feel seen, supported, and understood."

4. De-identify: "Their criticism isn't the full picture of who I am."

5. Express: Reflect. Vent. Reconnect with what you're proud of.

6. Integrate: "I can take feedback and still protect my self-worth."

Worried About Their Reaction

What Your Brain Does: You're afraid to share something important.

"They'll freak out."

"They won't get it."

"This will blow up."

6 Steps

1. Acknowledge: "I feel scared and tense."

2. Accept: "This is big for me—no wonder I'm nervous."

3. Understand: "I'm craving emotional safety and understanding."

4. De-identify: "Being afraid of conflict doesn't mean I'm doing something wrong."

5. Express: Practice what you want to say or write it out first.

6. Integrate: "My voice matters—and I can choose how and when to use it."

Not Being Allowed to Go Out

What Your Brain Does: You get told "no," and it stings.

"They don't trust me."

"I can't do anything."

"They want to control me."

6 Steps

1. Acknowledge: "I feel frustrated and powerless."

2. Accept: "I was hoping for freedom—this feels limiting."

3. Understand: "This is showing a need for autonomy and trust."

4. De-identify: "This rule doesn't define my independence."

5. Express: Have a calm convo later. Journal what freedom means to you.

6. Integrate: "I'm learning how to advocate for myself—even when I don't get my way."

Remember, these steps help you move through emotions with self-awareness instead of shame. Every time you pause to process like this, you're training your brain to respond, not just react—and that's emotional strength.

Chapter 2 Wrap-Up: From Pain to Power

Here's what we explored:

Emotional pain isn't just something to get over. It's a signal. A message. A doorway into something deeper.

When that pain goes unprocessed, it builds up like stuffing more and more into a backpack you carry every day. It starts shaping how you think, how you react, and how you connect with others.

When your thoughts begin looping around the pain, the emotions grow heavier. Each loop adds more weight.

The shift happens when you stop turning away from your feelings and start paying attention to them.

We broke down the **6-step emotional reset**. A way to move through pain while staying grounded in yourself:

Acknowledge what you're feeling
Accept it with compassion
Understand the deeper need behind it
De-identify from the stories your brain is telling
Express it in a way that helps it move
Integrate what you've learned along the way

Each time you practice this, something strong begins to grow inside you:

Emotional strength
Self-trust
The ability to feel deeply and still stay steady

As the pain begins to soften, something else becomes more visible.

Stillness. Presence. A deeper version of you that's always been there.

In Chapter 3, we begin stepping into that space. Not to erase anything you've felt, but to sit with life as it is, and find the kind of freedom that doesn't need to be chased. It's already here. And now, you'll know how to meet it.

Quote: "Not everything that is faced can be changed. But nothing can be changed until it is faced." James Baldwin
Song: "I Am Light" India.Arie

Chapter Three

Moving into the Now

Introduction: From Emotional Pain to Awakening

In Chapter 1, we talked about how your thoughts and ego shape the way you see the world, and how mindfulness helps you step back from the noise.

In Chapter 2, we explored emotional pain. How it builds up, lingers, and affects the way you think, feel, and react.

Now we're taking the next step.

What do you do after you've felt the pain? You learn to let it go.

When life gets tough, whether it's heartbreak, stress, or anxiety about the future, it's easy to get stuck in your head. You replay the past. You worry about what's next. You try to control everything.

Here's the truth.
You can't change yesterday.
You can't predict tomorrow.
The only moment you can live in, the only place real peace exists, is right now.

1. The Time Trap: Why Your Mind Keeps You Anywhere *But* Here

Your brain is kind of like a time traveler. One minute it's reliving something cringey from three years ago, the next it's spinning out about something that hasn't even happened yet.

Meanwhile, the only thing that's *actually* real, the present moment, gets totally ignored.

Here's the wild part.
The past is just a memory.
The future hasn't happened yet.
The present is the only thing that's actually real.

Think about that. This moment right now is the only place life is ever actually happening. Everything else is just a story in your head.

Two Types of Time: Clock Time vs. Psychological Time

To understand why we get stuck outside the present, it helps to know that we experience time in two very different ways. There's the practical, measured time that helps us navigate our days, and then there's the emotional, story-driven time that often traps us.

1. Clock Time (The Helpful Kind)

Keeping track of appointments
Knowing when class starts
Planning your day
Setting goals

This kind of time helps you function. It keeps life moving.

2. Psychological Time (The Messy Kind)

Replaying what went wrong
Worrying about what might happen
Creating entire stress movies in your head

This kind of time? It pulls you out of the now and traps you in stories, stories that feel real, but aren't.

Your Brain's Two Favorite Time Zones

Past Mode

→ "Why did I do that?"
→ "I should've known better."
→ "Everything was better back then..."

Future Mode

→ "What if I mess this up?"
→ "What if they leave?"
→ "What if I fail?"

Remember: The past is over, the future hasn't happened, and the present is all there is. This moment is where your power lives.

Breaking Free from the Time Trap

You don't have to stop thinking about the past or future completely, but you *can* stop getting stuck there.

Use Clock Time to stay grounded

• Plan what you can

• Show up for what matters

• Keep promises to yourself

Let go of Psychological Time traps

• Don't keep replaying old pain

• Catch yourself in "what if" spirals

• Stay curious, not panicked, about what's ahead

2. Understanding the Mind's Escape Tactics

Why You Keep Time-Traveling (Without Meaning To)

So now you know: the only real moment is now.

But here's the catch. Sometimes your brain hates staying here.

The second life feels even a little uncomfortable, your mind hits the eject button. It doesn't want to feel awkward or unsure or exposed, so it does what it thinks will protect you: it time-travels.

Back to the past. Forward into the future. Anywhere but here.

It's not trying to hurt you. It thinks it's helping. But instead, it pulls you away from what's real and into mental movies that aren't true, and that's where the spiral begins.

Let's look at what that looks like in everyday life.

1. The Social Media Spiral

When Scrolling Becomes a Mental Time Machine

You open Instagram just to pass time. Suddenly you're knee-deep in an existential crisis about your body, your life, and your self-worth.

The Scroll Begins

5:43 PM – Open Instagram
5:44 PM – See influencer's perfect gym selfie
5:45 PM – Brain goes into panic mode

Your Brain's Time-Travel Route

Past: "Remember when I felt so awkward at that beach party?"
Present: Mindlessly scrolling
Future: "I'll never look like that. I'm always going to be the 'before' picture."

What's Actually Happening

You're just chilling on your bed, phone in hand.
Your brain's version? A highlight-reel comparison meltdown.

The Time Trap Breakdown

0% of your thoughts are in the present
50% replaying past insecurities
50% spiraling about the future

Moment of Truth

You're not failing, ugly, or doomed. You're literally just scrolling.
The trap isn't the app—it's what your brain is doing while you scroll.

2. Test Anxiety Tornado

When Studying Becomes a Disaster Movie

You open your notes to study. Two pages in, you're convinced your entire future is toast.

The Study Session

6:15 PM – Open textbook
6:16 PM – Skim the first page
6:17 PM – Brain goes DEFCON 1

Your Brain's Time-Travel Route

Past: "I bombed that last quiz."
Present: Sitting with your notes
Future: "I'm going to fail this class, and my future is over."

What's Actually Happening

You're reading. Just reading.
But your brain's writing an Oscar-nominated academic tragedy.

The Time Trap Breakdown

0% about what you're learning now
50% stuck in past failures
50% forecasting doom

Moment of Truth

You're not failing or doomed. You're studying.
The trap isn't the test—it's your brain hijacking the moment.

3. Friend Drama Time Machine

When a Delayed Text Feels Like Rejection

You send a text. No response. Your brain fills in every blank.

The Text Timeline

7:12 PM – Send message
7:14 PM – No reply
7:15 PM – Brain meltdown

Your Brain's Time-Travel Route

Past: "Remember when they were annoyed last time?"
Present: Staring at the screen
Future: "They hate me. This friendship is over."

What's Actually Happening

They're probably just busy. Your brain? Hosting a one-person pity party.

The Time Trap Breakdown

0% rooted in the moment
50% replaying past fears
50% inventing rejection fantasies

Moment of Truth

You're not being ghosted. You're just waiting.
The trap isn't the delay—it's the movie your brain made in response.

4. Family Expectations Wormhole

When a Conversation Becomes a Lifetime of Disappointment

Your parents casually ask about college or career stuff. Suddenly, you're spiraling into "I'm a failure" territory.

The Conversation Timeline:

8:00 PM – Dinner table chat
8:01 PM – Future comes up
8:02 PM – Brain goes full meltdown

Your Brain's Time-Travel Route:

Past: "They've always expected more from me."
Present: Listening to a question
Future: "I'll never meet their expectations. I'm letting everyone down."

What's Actually Happening:

You're talking. That's it.
But your brain's filming a generational disappointment documentary.

The Time Trap Breakdown:

0% focused on the now
50% stuck in old pressure
50% panicking about future failure

Moment of Truth

You're not a failure. You're just having a convo.
The trap isn't their question—it's how your mind interprets it.

5. Future Career Panic

When a School Project Feels Like a Lifetime of Doom

You sit down to do an assignment. Ten minutes later, you're questioning your entire future.

The Project Timeline

9:00 PM – Open laptop
9:01 PM – Start typing
9:02 PM – Existential crisis

Your Brain's Time-Travel Route

Past: "I've always struggled with this."
Present: Working
Future: "I'm never going to succeed."

What's Actually Happening

You're literally doing homework.
But your brain? Filming the documentary "How It All Fell Apart."

The Time Trap Breakdown

0% about the current task
50% dredging up old stress
50% projecting failure

Moment of Truth

You're not doomed. You're just working.
The trap isn't the assignment—it's the fear your brain wrapped around it.

This Is What the Mind Does

Your brain time-travels to avoid discomfort. But the real discomfort isn't in the moment. It's in the story your brain is telling about the moment.

You don't have to live in those stories. You can come back. To this breath. This step. This second. And when you do, you're free.

The Time-Travel Check-In: A Daily Practice

Now that you understand how your mind slips away from the present moment, let's practice catching it in the act. This simple exercise helps you identify when you're time-traveling and gently bring yourself back to now.

How It Works

Three times a day, pause and ask yourself these questions:

1. Where Is My Mind Right Now?

- Am I mentally in the past? (Replaying, regretting, reminiscing)

- Am I mentally in the future? (Worrying, planning, fantasizing)

- Am I actually here, in this moment?

2. What's My Time-Travel Pattern?

Notice which direction your mind tends to go:

- **Past-focused:** "I keep thinking about what happened..."

- **Future-focused:** "I'm worried about what might happen..."

- **Ping-pong:** "I'm bouncing between past regrets and future fears..."

3. What's Actually Happening Right Now?

Take a moment to notice:

- What can you see?

- What can you hear?

- What can you feel physically?

- What are you actually doing in this moment?

4. The Reality Check

Compare your mental movie with what's actually happening:

- "My mind is telling me _________."

- "But right now, I'm just _________."

Track Your Time-Travel Patterns

Try this quick chart for one week. You might start to see patterns in when and how your mind time-travels.

Time of Day	Where Was My Mind?	What Triggered It?	What Was Actually Happening?
Morning	Future: Stressing about presentation	Saw calendar notification	Just brushing my teeth
Afternoon	Past: Replaying awkward conversation	Got a text from that person	Just sitting in class
Evening	Future: Worrying about college apps	Dad asked about deadlines	Just eating dinner

The Time-Travel Tracker: Blank Worksheet

Time of Day	Where Was My Mind?	What Triggered It?	What Was Actually Happening?
Morning			
Afternoon			
Evening			

Why This Works

Each time you catch yourself time-traveling, you're building awareness. And awareness is the first step to freedom from these mental patterns.

You don't need to judge yourself for time-traveling. Everyone's mind does it. The goal isn't to never time-travel. The goal is to notice when you do, and gently guide yourself back to now.

This simple practice helps you:

- Identify your specific time-travel patterns

- Create a pause between thought and reaction

- Develop the ability to return to the present

- Build the mental muscle of presence

3. The Problem with Avoiding the Present

Now that you can identify when your mind is time-traveling and practice bringing it back, let's look at why we avoid the present moment in the first place. Because once you understand the why, staying present becomes much easier.

Let's be real. Escaping feels good. Whether it's zoning out on TikTok, rehashing old convos, or procrastinating like it's your side hustle, avoidance gives you that temporary "ahhh" feeling.

But it doesn't actually fix anything.

Avoidance delays discomfort. It doesn't relieve it. And that's the difference. Avoidance and presence are easy to confuse, especially when both can involve rest. But they come from two very different places.

Presence is a choice to stay aware. It can mean sitting still, taking a break, or doing absolutely nothing, but doing it with intention. You're letting your mind and body settle without pushing your feelings away.

Avoidance, on the other hand, is when you distract yourself to escape what you feel. You keep busy or go numb, hoping the emotion disappears on its own. But instead of fading, it hides, and eventually comes back louder.

What Avoidance Looks Like IRL

Not sure if you're avoiding the present? Here's how it sneaks in.

Situation	What You Think You're Doing	What's Actually Happening	What It Felt Like Later	What Ended Up Happening
Scrolling for hours	"Just relaxing"	Avoiding stress or overwhelm	Drained, zoned out	Stress returned as soon as you stopped scrolling
Staying "super busy"	"Being productive"	Avoiding stillness or tough feelings	Tired but unsatisfied	Emotions hit harder once you slowed down
Bingeing Netflix	"I deserve a break"	Avoiding sadness, boredom, or anxiety	Numb, restless	Emptiness returned once it was over
Cancelling plans	"I'm just tired"	Avoiding social discomfort or fear of rejection	Disconnected or regretful	Still felt left out and uneasy
Cleaning everything	"Getting stuff done"	Avoiding mental clutter by focusing on physical space	Slight relief, but tension stayed	Mental mess waited right outside the tidy room
Going quiet or ghosting	"I need space"	Avoiding conflict or emotional vulnerability	Calm at first, then isolated	Feelings got stronger and harder to name

Reminder: Avoidance is not bad or shameful. It's simply a habit. And habits can change. The goal is not to eliminate distraction completely. The goal is to notice it sooner and choose presence more often.

Is It Avoidance or Presence? A Guided Check-In

Use these questions to reflect on a moment when you were resting, distracting, or pulling away. The goal isn't to judge yourself, but to notice the difference between escape and awareness.

1. What were you doing?
Describe the situation or activity. (Example: Scrolling TikTok, cancelling plans, watching Netflix, cleaning, etc.)

2. What did you tell yourself you were doing?
What was your mental explanation or justification? (Example: "I'm just relaxing," "I deserve this," "I'm too tired.")

3. What were you actually avoiding, if anything?
Was there a feeling, thought, or situation you didn't want to face? (Example: anxiety, sadness, overwhelm, fear of conflict, pressure to perform)

4. How did you feel afterward?
Did you feel more grounded and clear? Or drained, restless, or disconnected?

5. What ended up happening?
Did the emotion or discomfort go away? Or did it come back stronger later?

6. Looking back—was it presence or avoidance?
Were you choosing to be with yourself... or trying to escape something?

4. Letting Go of Psychological Time

Now that you've seen how the mind pulls you away from the present through distraction, overthinking, and avoidance, this next step brings everything together: **letting go.**

Letting go is the process of releasing the stories your mind creates about the past and future. It helps you return to the here and now, where life is actually happening.

When you live in psychological time, your thoughts drift elsewhere. You may find yourself replaying conversations, imagining what might happen, or trying to manage things that are not even here yet. These thoughts often feel urgent and important. They create tension and keep your nervous system on edge.

Letting go softens that grip. Instead of trying to stop your thoughts, you simply notice them and come back to the present. You reconnect with what is real and immediate.

Letting go does not mean forgetting. It does not mean giving up. It means becoming aware of what your mind is doing and gently guiding your attention back to now.

Let go of the need to control everything. Step back into the present, where your real life is waiting.

What This Looks Like in Real Life

Letting go sounds simple. But it feels different when you are in the middle of a social media spiral, stressing about a test, or overthinking a delayed text. This is where the practice becomes real.

When you catch yourself reacting automatically, flooded with thoughts and emotions that feel too big for the moment, this is your chance.

This is your reminder to pause, breathe, and shift.
From spiraling to steady. From stuck to open. From fear to clarity.

Let's look at what letting go can look like in everyday moments.

1. Social Media Spiral: Breaking the Comparison Trap

Practicing Letting Go: Scrolling through social media can feel like a break, then it turns into a spiral of self-doubt. You compare your real life to someone else's highlight reel.

Letting go is releasing the belief that you have to be flawless to be worthy.

What It Looks Like:

- Catch yourself mid-scroll and remember: these are curated moments, not full lives.

- Let go of the need for likes and approval.

- Your path is your own. It does not need to look like anyone else's.

2. Test Anxiety Tornado: Easing Academic Pressure

Practicing Letting Go: A tough exam can bring up fears of failure and pressure to get everything right.

Letting go is recognizing that your grades do not define your worth.

What It Looks Like:

- A bad grade is not the end. You are learning, not performing.

- Let go of the need to control every outcome.

- Focus on what is in front of you and give it your best effort.

3. Friend Drama Time Machine: Calming Social Chaos

Practicing Letting Go: A delayed text can trigger stories of rejection and disconnection.

Letting go is learning to sit with uncertainty without jumping to conclusions.

What It Looks Like:

- A delayed reply is not a rejection. Take a breath.

- Let go of the urge to seek constant reassurance.

- Trust the connection you have built.

4. Family Expectations Wormhole: Walking Your Own Path

Practicing Letting Go: Conversations about your future may bring up doubt or guilt.

Letting go is honoring your own path, even when it feels different from what others expect.

What It Looks Like:

- You are not a disappointment for dreaming differently.

- Let go of the need for approval.

- Trust your voice and let your direction unfold in its own time.

5. Future Career Panic: Embracing the Unknown

Practicing Letting Go: A single assignment can stir fears about your whole future.

Letting go is allowing space for the unknown without needing every answer.

What It Looks Like:

- You are figuring it out, and that is enough.

- Let go of the belief that you need a perfect plan.

- Growth takes time. Your path will reveal itself step by step.

Two Practices for Letting Go

1. Tangible Letting Go: A Physical Release Ritual

What It Is: This is your chance to take the emotional junk that's been weighing you down like stress, fear, resentment, pressure, and literally destroy it.

You're not just thinking "I'm letting go." You're doing it.

How It Works

1. Identify What's Been Dragging You Down

Ask yourself: "What have I been carrying that I'm ready to release?" Be specific. Whether it's:

- "I'm scared I'll fail this class"

- "I feel like I have to be perfect"

- "I'm still mad about what they said"

Name it. Own it. Get clear about what you're letting go.

2. Write It Down & Tear It Up

Grab a small piece of paper. Write the thought, fear, or story you're holding on to. Then: Tear it up. Throw it out. As you do, imagine that thought or emotion leaving your system.

3. Breathe & Let It Be

Take a slow, deep breath. Feel what it's like to no longer carry that weight. Tell yourself: "I've let this go now." You might not feel 100% lighter right away but you've done something real. You've taken a step.

Here's why turning a mental release into a physical act is so powerful.

Anchors the Mind

Telling yourself "I'm over it" sounds nice... but your brain might not buy it. Physically doing something—like tearing up a piece of paper with your fear written on it—sends a much louder message: We're done here.

Makes It Real

We're wired to respond to what we can see and touch. A physical act gives you a solid, memorable moment to say, "Yeah, I actually moved forward."

Gives You Closure

Think about breakups: deleting photos, trashing an old playlist, tossing a hoodie. It stings, but it also helps. That simple act says, "I'm done holding this."

In short: Physical release = mental reset. It turns vague intentions into real movement.

2. Healing Through Loving-Kindness Meditation

Loving-Kindness Meditation (LKM) might sound soft or even a little woo-woo at first—sending good vibes to yourself and even people who hurt you? Sounds wild.

This isn't about pretending everything's okay. It's about releasing the resentment that's been poisoning your peace.

It's not about them. It's about you choosing to stop carrying the pain.

How to Practice Loving-Kindness Meditation

1. Find a Quiet Spot

Sit somewhere comfortable. Close your eyes. Take a few deep breaths. Imagine a warm, glowing light around you—safe, peaceful, calming.

2. Start with Yourself

Repeat these phrases in your mind:

May I be happy.
May I be healthy.
May I be safe.
May I be at peace.

Let the words sink in. You don't have to believe them 100%. Just let yourself hear them.

3. Send Kindness to Someone You Trust

Picture someone who supports you like a friend, a mentor, a family member. Visualize the warm light surrounding them.

Repeat:

May you be happy.
May you be healthy.

May you be safe.
May you be at peace.

4. Expand It to the World

Now, picture the light growing.

Imagine it surrounding people you know, strangers you'll never meet, and anyone who's ever felt pain.

Repeat:

May all beings be happy.
May all beings be healthy.
May all beings be safe.
May all beings be at peace.

5. The Optional Step: If and When You're Ready

This next part isn't required. If it doesn't feel right for you right now, you can skip it or come back another time.

Think of someone who hurt you. Maybe they let you down. Maybe they made you feel small, invisible, or not enough.

You don't have to forgive them. You don't even have to like them.

This isn't about them. It's about you not having to carry the weight of what happened any longer.

If it feels okay, picture a soft light surrounding them—not because they earned it, but because you're choosing peace for yourself.

You can say to yourself:
May you be happy.
May you be healthy.
May you be safe.
May you be at peace.

If that feels like too much, try:

May *I* be free.

May *I* feel peace.

Let this be something you return to when you're ready. You set the pace. You're in control.

When to Use This Practice

LKM helps release pain that talking or journaling alone can't always reach. Use it when:

- A fight still stings

- A betrayal keeps replaying

- A hard memory still has a grip

- You feel disconnected from yourself

What This Practice Actually Does

You stop giving energy to people who don't deserve it
You take your power back from old wounds
You choose peace over resentment
You heal without needing closure from anyone else

Final Thoughts: Letting Go Is For You

Letting go is not about forgetting the past or pretending things did not hurt. Letting go is not about them. It is about choosing to come back to yourself with softness and care. It is about giving yourself the freedom to live fully in the present.

You may need to return to these practices again and again. That is not a sign of failure. It is part of the process. It is part of the healing.

Chapter 3 Wrap-Up: Moving Into the Now

Here's what we've unlocked:

Your mind is a time traveler. Constantly flipping between the past and future to avoid discomfort.

Psychological time (the stories you tell yourself about what was or what might be) can trap you in overthinking, avoidance, and emotional spirals.

But presence? Presence is your way out. It's the only place healing, clarity, and real freedom actually live.

We explored how to stop mentally time-traveling and come back to the only moment that's real: right now.

We also introduced two powerful tools:

Tangible Release – A physical ritual to help your brain feel the letting go, not just think it
Loving-Kindness Meditation – A practice to help you release old wounds and choose peace, even when forgiveness feels impossible

Now that you've landed in the present... what do you do with it?

That's where we're going next.

In Chapter 4, we press pause on the noise of life—school, expectations, the endless to-do list—and ask a bigger question:

What actually matters?

Quote: "Forever is composed of nows." Emily Dickinson
Song: "Let It All Go" Birdy and Rhodes

Chapter Four

Real You, Real Life

Introduction: Pressing Pause to Wake Up

You've just made it through one of the most powerful shifts. Learning how to stop running from the present moment.

In Chapter 3, we explored how your mind time-travels to avoid discomfort and how letting go helps you reconnect with what's real. So now that you've learned how to *be here*, really here, you might be wondering: **What now?**

Because even when you're grounded in the now, there can still be a quiet emptiness that creeps in during the in-between moments.

That still, subtle voice that whispers:

"Is this really it?"

You go to class. You keep up with texts. You chase the next grade, the next goal, the next "good job."

And yet... something feels off.

That's not just boredom or burnout. That's your *real self* trying to get your attention.

Back in Chapter 1, we talked about the **ego**. The mental costume you wear to fit in, achieve, protect, and prove. It's the version of you shaped by expectations, comparison, and fear. Not fake, but not fully you either.

If you never stop to question it, you end up living life from that surface-level identity, what we called the *fake ID*. And when life is built around a false self, even your wins can feel hollow.

So this chapter is your invitation to **press pause** on that identity.

To ask:

"Who am I underneath all this?" "What actually matters to me?"

This is about what your life feels like when it's rooted in something true. Something deeper than hustle, image, or approval.

You can achieve many things and still feel unsettled inside. You can succeed on paper and feel uncertain in your own skin. When what you're working toward doesn't reflect who you truly are, it may not bring the peace you're looking for.

In this chapter, we'll:

Unpack why external success might leave you feeling disconnected
Explore how society's idea of happiness can actually pull you further from yourself
Learn how reconnecting with your true identity brings clarity, direction, and peace
Help you build a life that feels good, not just one that looks good

Real peace and real purpose isn't something you chase. It's something you return to when you get quiet enough to hear your own truth.

This is not about fixing yourself. It's about beginning a deeper, more honest relationship with who you already are. And from that place of connection, things begin to shift.

1. Real Life vs. Life Situations: The Core Difference

You live through a lot of situations. Tests. Breakups. Awkward moments. Family pressure. Deadlines. Fights. Wins. Losses. Every day brings something new.

And when you're in it, when it feels intense or personal or overwhelming, it's easy to mistake what's happening around you for who you are.

But here's the truth:

Life situations are what you go through. Real life is the you who goes through them.

This is one of the most important distinctions you can learn.

A life situation is a temporary experience. It's something happening right now, or something that happened in the past. It could be an argument, a failed test, a moment of self-doubt, or a phase where everything just feels off. These situations can feel heavy, frustrating, even defining in the moment.

But they aren't you.

You are the constant in all of it. You are the one who experiences, reflects, responds, learns, and moves forward. That's your real life. Not the events themselves, but the person you are within and beyond them.

Life Situations vs. Real Life

You've seen throughout this book how easily your brain can spiral when something hard happens. Let's revisit some of those situations from earlier chapters. This chart will help you tell the difference between a temporary moment and your deeper truth.

Life Situation (Temporary)	What Your Mind Might Say	Real Life (Who You Are)
1. Left on Read	"They're ignoring me." "I'm too much." Pause. That's anxiety—not truth.	You are worthy of connection and belonging'
2. Outfit Comment	"Why did I wear this?" "I shouldn't have tried." Pause. That's insecurity—not truth.	You are allowed to express yourself and take up space
3. Said Something Weird	"They probably think I'm awkward." "I always say the wrong thing." Pause. That's self-doubt—not truth.	You are learning how to connect and communicate
4. Waking Up in a Funk	"What's wrong with me?" "I should feel better." Pause. That's heaviness—not truth.	You are still whole, even on low-energy days
5. Snapping and Regretting It	"I ruin everything." "They'll never forgive me." Pause. That's guilt—not truth.	You are capable of growth, repair, and self-awareness
6. Decision Paralysis	"What if I mess this up?" "I can't trust myself." Pause. That's fear—not truth.	You are capable of choice and momentum
7. Bombed a Quiz	"I'm not smart enough." "Why even try?" Pause. That's discouragement—not truth.	You are capable of learning, improving, and succeeding
8. Procrastination Spiral	"I always mess around." "I'm falling behind." Pause. That's avoidance—not truth.	You are still moving forward, even in small steps
9. Needing Help but Not Asking	"They'll think I'm dumb." "I should already know this." Pause. That's shame—not truth.	You are brave for asking and deserving of support
10. Parent Criticizes You	"I'm not enough." "Why do I even try?" Pause. That's hurt—not truth.	You are more than one person's opinion
11. Worried About Their Reaction	"This will blow up." "They won't understand." Pause. That's fear—not truth.	You are allowed to speak your truth and set boundaries
12. Not Being Allowed to Go Out	"They don't trust me." "They want to control me." Pause. That's frustration—not truth.	You are still growing in independence and self-advocacy

Now that you've learned the difference between your real self and the situations around you, let's talk about how to actually stay connected to that deeper self, especially when things feel intense.

The Centering Check-In

How to Stay Grounded in Who You Are (Even When Life Feels Chaotic)

When something stressful or emotional happens, your brain loves to turn it into a story about who you are:

"I failed, so I must be a failure."
"They left, so I must not be lovable."
"I messed up, so I must not be good enough."

This check-in helps you interrupt that spiral and reconnect with your real self. Not the false identity created by a single moment.

Step 1: Name What's Happening

Get honest. But keep it neutral. No drama, no judgment. Just facts.

"I got a bad grade."
"They didn't text back."
"I felt awkward in that group."

Reminder: This is something you're experiencing. It's not who you are.

Step 2: Separate the Situation from Your Identity

Ask yourself:

"What is this moment trying to convince me about who I am?"
"Is that actually true—or just a reaction?"

Then gently affirm what you know is still true:

"I got a bad grade... but I'm still capable and curious."
"They didn't reply... but I'm still worthy of connection."
"I felt off today... but I'm still growing and learning."

You are not the scene. You are the whole story.

Step 3: Zoom Out to Regain Perspective

Ask:

"What's the bigger picture?"
"Will this still matter a year from now?"

This step moves you from self-blame to self-compassion. It helps you respond instead of react.

Centering Script: Say It Out Loud or Write It Down

Here's a script you can speak, journal, or even whisper in your head to re-ground yourself when you're spinning out:

"This is a moment. It's not my identity.
I'm allowed to feel what I feel, but I don't have to turn it into a story about who I am.
I am not this grade. I am not this comment. I am not this mistake.
I am still growing. I am still worthy. I am still me."

Use it when you're overwhelmed or adapt it to make it yours. The more you practice, the easier it becomes to stay connected to the real you.

2. Finding Your Purpose: Beyond Life Situations

In the last section, we explored the difference between what happens to you and who you are underneath it all. Now we're moving into something just as important. Your purpose.

Purpose is not a place you arrive. It is not something you suddenly figure out or something you earn. It begins quietly. It shows up in what feels meaningful to you, and it becomes clearer the more you understand yourself.

When It Feels Like Everyone Else Has It Figured Out

Sometimes it feels like everyone around you is moving faster. Posting big moments, reaching milestones, and getting recognized. You might see:

- Someone getting into their top college

- A classmate winning awards or scholarships

- A friend always posting perfect photos or exciting updates

It's easy to start wondering, *"Am I doing enough?"* or *"Should I have it all figured out too?"*

That pressure can push you to look for purpose in what gets attention. Likes, praise, achievements. These things might feel exciting in the moment, but they don't always reflect what's real for you.

You don't have to chase what looks impressive. Meaning isn't always loud. It often shows up in quiet ways. Like helping a friend, getting lost in a creative project, or feeling proud after doing something hard.

Purpose grows when you stay connected to what feels true, not what looks good from the outside. Your timeline is your own. You are allowed to move at your pace and shape a life that fits who you are becoming.

Practice: Intuitive Writing for Purpose

This isn't about having your whole life figured out. It's about pausing, listening in, and letting your deeper self speak up.

How to Start

Find a quiet space. Grab a notebook or open your Notes app. Set a timer for 15 minutes. Answer the questions below—freely, honestly, and without overthinking.

Questions to Explore Your Purpose (with examples)

1. What makes me feel most alive?

   - Dancing with my friends

   - Getting absorbed in drawing

   - Being in nature, especially near water

Your answer:

2. What would I do if no one was judging me?

   - Start a YouTube channel

   - Wear exactly what I want

   - Share my poems or music

Your answer:

3. What do I find myself thinking about, even when I'm busy?

   - Mental health and how people cope

   - Music and playlists

- How to make people laugh or feel seen

Your answer:

4. When was the last time I felt truly at peace—or truly excited? What was I doing?

- Laying in the grass listening to music

- Finishing a story I was proud of

- Helping a friend through something hard

Your answer:

5. What problems in the world actually bother me enough to want to help?

- People feeling alone or unseen

- Injustice or unfair treatment

- Lack of emotional education in schools

Your answer:

Then Go Deeper

6. Why does this matter to me?

- Because I've felt invisible, and I don't want others to feel that way.

- Because when I'm creating, I feel like my most honest self.

- Because connection makes life feel real.

Your answer:

7. What moments stand out in my memory?

- The time a teacher told me my writing made them cry.

- When I stayed up late helping a friend through something heavy.

- That day I sat by the ocean and felt completely calm.

Your answer:

8. How could I follow or expand this feeling?

- Share one piece of writing, even if it's just on a small platform.

- Look for volunteer work that helps people feel supported.

- Make time every week to do something that brings me peace.

Your answer:

Now What?

Look back at what you wrote. Are there any patterns or feelings that show up more than once? Is there a thread that connects a few of your answers? You don't need to figure everything out right now. Just notice what stands out. Sometimes purpose isn't a big plan. Sometimes it's a quiet pull toward what already lights you up. Keep listening. Keep following the spark.

3. Recognizing False Pursuits of Happiness

Chasing Happiness in All the Wrong Places

In the last section, we talked about discovering purpose by tuning into your authentic self.

But there's another part of the picture that's just as important and just as easy to get wrong:

Happiness doesn't come from external success, no matter how much the world tells you it does.

Just like purpose, real happiness starts within. But somewhere along the way, happiness became a prize. A finish line. Something to chase, buy, or earn. Like you'll finally feel "okay" once you've unlocked the right grades, friends, body, relationship, lifestyle.

But those external "fixes"? They don't last.
They give you a burst of excitement. A high that fades fast.
And once it's gone, you're left searching for the next hit.

The Firework Effect: Why External Highs Fade

Think of a firework: It lights up the sky with intensity, color, and sound... ...and then it's gone.

That's what it feels like when you:

- Get the perfect grade

- Hit a social media milestone

- Buy the trendiest outfit

It feels amazing for a moment.

But it doesn't stay. And without something deeper anchoring you, you end up chasing the next high.

Again. And again. And again.

The Happiness Traps

Places where you might get stuck:

Social Media Validation

- Counting likes as proof of your worth

- Feeling like a perfect post = personal success

- Watching your follower count like a scoreboard for your value

Academic Achievement Spiral

- Believing the "right" school will fix your self-doubt

- Letting your GPA define your entire identity

- Thinking success = happiness

Relationship Rescue Fantasy

- Hoping love will heal your sadness

- Wanting a partner to prove you're lovable

- Seeking perfection in dating to fill what feels empty

Aesthetic = Identity Trap

- Thinking new clothes or trends will finally make you feel confident

- Believing your worth is tied to how "put together" you look

- Dressing for attention instead of expression

Main Character Syndrome

- Trying to make every moment look cinematic

- Feeling like your life has to be exciting 24/7

- Comparing your quiet days to someone else's drama

Friendship Performance

- Hanging out just for the photos

- Being "on" all the time to seem fun or easygoing

- Hiding your true feelings to avoid rocking the boat

Glow-Up Myth

- Believing a physical transformation will "fix" your self-esteem

- Tying happiness to weight loss, clear skin, or muscles

- Waiting for a "new you" to start living your life

Comparison Loop

- Measuring your success by someone else's timeline

- Thinking "I should be there by now"

- Ignoring your growth because someone else seems ahead

Overthinking Everything

- Replaying every conversation to spot what you did wrong

- Doubting compliments or kind gestures

- Being so deep in your head you miss the moment you're in

Family Approval Pressure

- Trying to live up to unspoken expectations

- Feeling like your choices don't matter if they aren't praised

- Believing that love equals performance

The Real Shift: From Achievement to Awareness

Trying to find happiness in things that don't last is like chasing a shadow. You keep moving, but you never actually catch what you're looking for. Real, lasting happiness doesn't come from the outside. It comes from inside. From a place of awareness, not achievement.

True happiness grows from:

Inner calm
Gratitude
Self-awareness
A connection to what genuinely matters to you

It's not about chasing. It's about choosing.

Choosing to:

- See the good that's already here

- Trust that you're already enough

- Slow down instead of sprinting toward some imaginary finish line

Gratitude as the Antidote

So how do you recognize the trap, and choose something more real?

You flip your focus.
Instead of obsessing over what's missing, you begin noticing what's already here.

That's where gratitude comes in.
Gratitude isn't just a feel-good habit. It's a mindset shift.

It gently pulls you out of scarcity and into presence.
It reminds you that life isn't something you earn. It's something you experience.

Practice: Gratitude Journaling

What It Is

A simple daily habit that helps you reconnect with the now and recognize what's already working in your life.

How To Do It

1. Set aside 2–5 minutes (morning or evening works best)

2. Write down 3–5 things you're grateful for

3. Big or small—everything counts

4. A deep laugh, a soft hoodie, a class that went surprisingly well

Prompts to Get You Started (with examples)

What made me smile today?

- My dog doing that weird tail-spin thing when I came home

- A friend sending me a meme that was *way* too accurate

- Hearing my favorite song come on shuffle during a stressful moment

Your answer:

Who showed me even a small act of kindness this week?

- A classmate who held the door open even though I was far away

- My sibling giving me the last slice of pizza (without a fight)

- A teacher who noticed I was off and checked in after class

Your answer:

What's something I usually take for granted that I'm thankful for right now?

- Having earbuds to tune out and reset during the day

- The group chat that always makes me laugh, even when I'm sad

- Being able to walk to the park when I need space to think

Your answer:

What You'll Start to Notice

A quieter mind
Less pressure to constantly "be better"
More peace, even when life feels uncertain

The Takeaway

Happiness isn't something you "get." It's something you realize and practice.

And the more you practice awareness, the more you:

- Stop measuring your worth by what you achieve

- Start appreciating who you already are

- Build a happiness that lasts. Not because life is perfect, but because you're present

Because here's the best part:

This kind of happiness doesn't depend on anything outside of you.
It lives in you already.
You just have to slow down, look in, and let it rise.

Chapter 4 Wrap-Up: Real Life, True Purpose, and Authentic Happiness

Here's what we uncovered:

Life situations are what you go through. Real life is the you who goes through them.

You learned to separate your identity from the chaos, and reconnect with something deeper and steadier inside you.

You explored how purpose isn't a destination, a title, or a plan.
It's a quiet knowing that comes from living in alignment with your values, your patterns, your passions.

You broke free from the trap of chasing happiness through grades, likes, relationships, or perfection and started shifting toward something more lasting: Gratitude. Presence. Meaning.

You practiced:

Intuitive Writing for Purpose – to tune in to your truth and what excites you beneath the noise
Gratitude Journaling – to stay grounded in what's already enough, instead of always reaching for more

The more you live from the inside out, not the outside in, the more real and peaceful your life becomes.

Up next: we bring this inner alignment into your relationships.

Quote: "You are not too late. You are right on time. Life has been waiting for you to show up exactly as you are." Donna Ashworth
Song: "Follow The Sun" Xavier Rudd

Chapter Five

Redefining Self in Relationships

Introduction: Inner Work Meets the Outer World

By now, you've done some of the deepest inner work there is. You've learned how to step back from your thoughts (Chapter 1), how to feel your emotions without being consumed by them (Chapter 2), how to let go of the past and come back to the present (Chapter 3), and how to uncover a sense of purpose that comes from within, not from achievements, appearances, or approval (Chapter 4).

But all of that growth doesn't stop with you alone in your room.

The real test? **Relationships.**

Because it's one thing to know who you are when it's quiet. It's another thing to *stay rooted in that truth* when you're surrounded by pressure, judgment, comparison, or even love.

In Chapter 4, we explored what it means to live in alignment with your truth. Now, the question becomes: **Can you stay true to yourself while staying connected to others?**

Most people think of personal growth as something that happens alone like on a mountaintop, in a journal, or during meditation.

But some of the *biggest* shifts happen in the everyday messiness of being human together:

- A conflict with a friend

- A crush that shakes your confidence

- A family argument that reopens old wounds

- A moment where you finally speak your truth, and aren't sure if they'll stay

These moments are mirrors. They reflect back not just how you feel about *others*, but how you feel about *yourself*.

So ask yourself:

- Am I constantly changing myself to fit in?

- Am I scared to say how I really feel?

- Am I relying on someone else to feel whole?

These aren't just social questions. They're **spiritual** ones.

This chapter is where everything you've learned so far gets put into practice—**in your connections**.

We'll explore how to:

- Drop the outdated roles you've outgrown

- Stay grounded even when you feel rejected or misunderstood

- Let go of emotional dependency

- Build real compassion for others and for yourself

1. The Relationship Mirror: How Connections Shape Who We Become

Different People, Different Yous

We've already explored the difference between your true self and the "fake ID" your ego creates. Now let's take it one step further. Into your relationships.

Think of yourself like a prism. You are one whole, complex being, and your light refracts in different ways depending on who you're around. Each relationship reflects a different color, angle, or tone of you. Some highlight your depth, others your humor or strength. These aren't false versions. They're shaped by connection, trust, and the space you're in.

But sometimes, the light gets filtered too much. Instead of reflecting who you are, you start adjusting to what you think others want. The version of you that shows up might be about safety or acceptance, but it can start to feel disconnected, like you're dimming instead of shining.

That version might be trying to avoid conflict, gain approval, or stay included. Still, if you feel more like you're performing than connecting, it's okay to pause and ask: what part of me feels unseen here?

Your full light is still there, even if others only reflect back a small part. You are whole, even when it feels like only one color is shining through.

The Invisible Agreement

Psychologists call this kind of shapeshifting an "invisible agreement," an unspoken contract about who you're expected to be around someone else.

Take Mia, for example. In her family, she's known as "the responsible one." She never causes drama, gets good grades, and keeps things running smoothly. This role wasn't something she chose. It formed naturally, especially as her younger siblings needed more attention. Being low-maintenance earned her praise.

But with her best friend Taylor, Mia is louder, sillier, more open to risks. The invisible agreement with Taylor makes space for a freer version of her to come through.

Then there's her new crush. Around them, Mia starts laughing at jokes she doesn't find funny, downplaying her opinions, and filtering herself constantly. That invisible agreement sounds more like: "Be appealing, not too much."

Three relationships. Three versions of Mia. None of them are fake. They are different refractions of her light. Each shaped by context, safety, and history.

The key is noticing when a version of you feels like just one narrow beam instead of your full spectrum. If a relationship only reflects one part of you, and leaves no room for the rest, you can pause and ask: is this still connected to who I really am?

You are a prism, not a performance. Your light is real, and it holds every color you are.

The Relationship Identity Trap

When your identity starts shifting, not from choice, but from fear, pressure, or habit, you begin to lose connection with your full self. Like light moving through a distorted prism, your truth gets bent in ways that no longer reflect who you are. This is the **Relationship Identity Trap**: a set of patterns that often begin as strengths, but over time, can hold you back if you're not aware of them.

The Chameleon Effect

What it is: Adapting so well to others that you lose track of your own preferences.
Real-life example: You're goofy with one group, serious with another, and quiet around your crush. Everyone likes you, but you start to feel like no one really *knows* you.
How it starts as a strength: You're emotionally intelligent. You pick up on what others need and help people feel comfortable around you. That's a gift.
Becomes a trap when: You always default to fitting in instead of speaking up. You say "yes" when you mean "no," or agree with things you don't believe.
Reminder: Your adaptability is powerful, but it's only a strength when it includes

you. The real you isn't the version that pleases everyone. It's the version you feel most at home in.

Relational Exhaustion

What it is: Feeling drained from constantly playing different roles to meet others' needs. **Real-life example:** You're the motivator for your friends, the calm one at home, and the supportive partner. You're strong, but inside, you're tired.

How it starts as a strength: You're dependable. People trust you. You're a steady presence when things get hard.

Becomes a trap when: You stop allowing space for your own struggles. You always show up for others but don't know how to ask for help.

Reminder: You don't have to be the strong one all the time. The version of you that needs care, rest, or a break is just as worthy and just as real.

The Approval Loop

What it is: Making choices based on what others will like instead of what feels meaningful to you.

Real-life example: You pick activities, clothes, even college plans based on what gets praise. You're constantly checking for likes, online and off.

How it starts as a strength: You're thoughtful. You know how to make others feel seen and included.

Becomes a trap when: You can't tell whether you're doing something for yourself or just for recognition. You lose touch with what truly matters to you.

Reminder: You already matter without proving anything. Approval feels good, but it isn't the same as purpose. Your inner compass deserves your trust.

Emotional Freezing

What it is: Shutting down or hiding your feelings to avoid drama or seem "easygoing."

Real-life example: Someone crosses a line, but you brush it off. You get left out, but you act like it's no big deal.

How it starts as a strength: You're calm under pressure. You don't make things harder than they need to be. That's stabilizing for others.

Becomes a trap when: You hide your feelings so well that even *you* stop recognizing them. No one knows what's actually going on inside.

Reminder: Your peacekeeping matters, but your pain matters too. Your emotions are not too much. You can be grounded *and* honest at the same time.

These patterns aren't flaws. They're strengths that have stretched beyond their balance.

You still hold the power to return to center.

Awareness is what helps you bring your full light back into the room.

Making Space for Authentic Connection

You've just explored how your light can get bent in ways that protect others but disconnect you from yourself. These patterns like the Chameleon Effect, Relational Exhaustion, the Approval Loop, and Emotional Freezing often begin as strengths. But when they go unchecked, they can keep your truth tucked away.

This next part is about making space for that truth to return. It's not about being the same in every relationship. It's about knowing what's real for you, so your relationships reflect who you are, not just who you've learned to be.

Ask yourself:

- Where do I feel most like myself?

- Where do I feel the need to edit or perform?

- Which parts of me rarely get seen, even by the people I'm closest to?

You don't have to reveal everything to everyone. Authenticity means being in touch with your truth, even if you choose not to share every part of it in every space. It's the difference between hiding who you are and holding it with care.

The Relationship Spectrum

Not every relationship feels the same. Some make you feel small or unsure. You might catch yourself holding back, staying quiet, or adjusting your personality just to keep the peace.

Others feel more neutral. You don't feel drained, but you're not fully seen either. There's not much tension, but also not much depth.

And then there are relationships that feel open and energizing. You feel more like yourself. You speak freely, laugh louder, and share more honestly. These connections don't just accept you. They help you grow.

You don't need every relationship to be deep or perfect. But paying attention to how you feel in each one helps you make clearer choices. It shows you where you feel safe to be real, and where you're still playing a role.

Small Moments of Truth

Bringing your full self into a relationship rarely happens in one big moment. It happens in small, quiet choices:

- Sharing something honest you usually keep hidden

- Saying "I don't agree with that" instead of nodding along

- Naming a boundary, even if your voice shakes

- Showing your full range. Messy, bright, unsure, curious

Each of these moments cracks open a little more space for you. Each one says, *"This is part of me too."*

Some relationships will stretch to meet you there. Others might not. That doesn't mean you failed. It means you're learning what fits your full light, and what doesn't.

And that's where the next part of your journey begins.

Self-Exploration Practice: *The "True Me in Relationships" Map*

This practice helps you explore how you show up in different relationships, notice where you feel most like yourself, and take small steps toward reconnecting with your full self.

Step 1: Map Your Relationship Selves

Create a list or chart with four parts for each relationship:

- **Relationship** – Who is this about? (e.g., friend, parent, teacher, crush)

- **How I Show Up** – What version of yourself do you express?

- **Why It Happens** – What fear, habit, or history might be shaping that?

- **Unbalanced Strength** – What strength might be overused or out of balance?

Relationship	How I Show Up	Why It Happens	Unbalanced Strength
Parents	Responsible, hides struggles	They worry easily; I don't want to stress them out	Independence, emotional control
Best Friend	Fun, supportive, avoids serious topics	I don't want to seem too heavy or make it awkward	Positivity, protection
Crush	Chill, agreeable	I'm afraid they won't like the "real me"	Flexibility, likability
Group Chat Friends	Peacemaker, stays neutral	I want to keep everyone happy	Harmony, conflict-avoidance
Teacher	Quiet, overly formal	Don't want to seem disrespectful or "too much"	Respect, self-restraint

Step 2: Spot the Invisible Agreements

Ask yourself for each relationship:

- What silent "rules" have I picked up about who I need to be?

- What feels off-limits to express?

Examples:

- "I have to be the strong one"

- "I can't show jealousy or insecurity"

- "I'm the funny one. I can't be serious"

- "They only like me when I'm chill"

Step 3: Reflect on the Relationship Spectrum

Look at the relationships in your life and ask yourself:

- In which ones do I feel most free to be my full self?

- In which ones do I find myself holding back or playing a role?

- Where do I feel supported, and where do I feel drained?

Arrange your relationships along a spectrum. From those where you feel the most open and real to those where you feel more limited or unseen.

You're not judging anyone here. You're simply noticing what kind of space each relationship makes for you, and what parts of you feel welcome (or not). This kind of clarity helps you show up more intentionally.

Step 4: Choose One Relationship to Explore

Pick a relationship that feels important, but where you've been holding back.

Ask yourself:

- What invisible rule would I like to gently break?

- What's one small action I could take to be a little more honest or whole?

Examples:

- Tell a friend you're actually not okay today.

- Say no to plans without over-explaining.

- Speak your actual opinion, even if it's different.

Step 5: Set an Authenticity Intention

Write a one-sentence intention to anchor how you want to show up in that relationship.

Try starting with:

- *"I'm choosing to..."*

- *"I allow myself to..."*

- *"I give myself permission to..."*

Examples:

- "I'm choosing to share more of what I really think, even if it's not always easy."

- "I allow myself to need rest instead of always being the strong one."

- "I give myself permission to be fully myself, even if it doesn't please everyone."

If Someone Doesn't Feel Ready for the Real You

As you grow and show more of your truth—your opinions, your emotions, your needs—some people might not know how to respond.

They may back off. Change the subject. Make you feel like you're asking for too much. This doesn't mean you're doing something wrong. It means they might not be ready.

Maybe they've gotten used to the version of you that stayed small to keep the peace. Maybe they're dealing with their own fears and don't know how to meet someone who's being honest.
Maybe closeness feels hard for them in ways you'll never fully see.

That can hurt. It's okay to feel that.
But it doesn't mean you should stop being real.

Let this be your reminder:

- You are not "too much" for being honest.

- You are not wrong for wanting to be seen.

- You are not difficult for showing up as yourself.

Some people may grow with you. Some won't. But the more you stay connected to your truth, the more you'll start to notice who feels safe to be around, and who asks you to dim your light just to stay close.

That kind of clarity is a gift. It helps you choose relationships that reflect who you are, not just who you've learned to be.

Let's look at some real-life moments where this can show up.

Parent Relationship

- **How I Show Up:** The high-achieving, low-maintenance one. I don't show struggle or ask for much.

- **Why It Happens:** I don't want to worry them, and I've always felt responsible for keeping things calm.

- **Unbalanced Strength:** Independence

- **Invisible Agreement:** "If I show my struggles, I'll disappoint them."

- **Authenticity Intention:** *I allow myself to ask for support when I need it. My vulnerability isn't a burden. It's part of being real.*

Friend Group

- **How I Show Up:** The advice-giver. I help everyone else, but rarely share what I'm going through.

- **Why It Happens:** I'm afraid of being seen as dramatic or making things about me.

- **Unbalanced Strength:** Empathy

- **Invisible Agreement:** "I'm the one who supports others. I shouldn't need support back."

- **Authenticity Intention:** *I'm choosing to share when I'm having a hard time. Real friendship goes both ways.*

Romantic Relationship

- **How I Show Up:** Easygoing, low-needs, never initiating tough conversations.

- **Why It Happens:** I'm afraid being too much will make them pull away.

- **Unbalanced Strength:** Flexibility

- **Invisible Agreement:** "If I express a need, I'll be seen as difficult."

- **Authenticity Intention:** *I give myself permission to speak up about what I feel and need. My needs are valid too.*

Teacher or Mentor

- **How I Show Up:** The polished one. I only show the final product, not the struggle.

- **Why It Happens:** I want to be seen as capable and together all the time.

- **Unbalanced Strength:** Discipline

- **Invisible Agreement:** "If I admit I'm stuck, I'll seem like I'm not good enough."

- **Authenticity Intention:** *I will ask for help when I need it. Learning is allowed to look messy.*

New Friendship

- **How I Show Up:** A filtered version. I hide some of my real interests and opinions.

- **Why It Happens:** I want to be liked and accepted quickly.

- **Unbalanced Strength:** Social awareness

- **Invisible Agreement:** "If I'm too weird or too honest, they won't want to be friends."

- **Authenticity Intention:** *I'm allowing myself to bring more of the real me into this friendship, even if it feels risky.*

Up Next

Now that you're learning to show up more authentically in relationships, we'll explore the next challenge: emotional dependency.

2. Moving Beyond Dependency: Finding Wholeness in Relationships

Understanding Emotional Dependency

It's natural to care deeply about the people in your life. Friendships, relationships, group chats. They matter. They shape how you feel, how you grow, and how you show up in the world.

So when someone doesn't text back, pulls away, or acts differently, it's normal to feel thrown off. A small comment or shift in tone can sting. That's human.

But sometimes, that care starts to carry more weight than you realize. Your confidence starts to shift based on how someone treats you. One message can change your whole mood. When someone pulls back, you start to feel unsure of yourself.

That's when emotional dependency can start to show up. It's when your sense of okay-ness begins to rely on someone else's attention, approval, or presence.

You still care. You still feel. But you don't lose yourself in it. That's the balance we're learning to build.

Why Dependency Happens

Emotional dependency often grows in places where connection felt hard to hold. Where feeling close didn't feel safe, stable, or consistent. Maybe you were praised for keeping it together or for not needing much. Maybe you were the one others leaned on, but no one really checked in on you. Maybe someone finally gave you attention, and it lit up something inside you that had been quiet for a long time.

When connection feels fragile or unpredictable, like it might disappear if you ask for too much, you start to hold on tightly. You shape yourself around what others need. You learn that feeling safe sometimes means being needed.

These experiences shape your response to closeness. They form emotional patterns that can feel hard to break. But those patterns aren't flaws. They're adaptations. And now, instead of blaming yourself, you get to look at them with honesty, care, and curiosity, not shame.

What Dependency Costs You

Dependency can feel like love. But underneath it is often fear. Fear of abandonment, fear of not being enough, fear that you'll lose your place in someone's life if you stop over-functioning, over-giving, or staying small.

Over time, the cost is heavy:

- You shrink yourself to stay close

- You silence your needs to avoid rocking the boat

- You read into every mood shift, every delay, every small sign of distance

- You start feeling like your peace, your confidence, and your identity live in someone else's hands

But your sense of self was never meant to belong to someone else. It lives in you. And it can stay steady, even when others shift.

To make this real, let's look at seven moments where dependency often sneaks in, and what it looks like to start stepping into self-trust instead.

7 Hidden Signs of Emotional Dependency

1. The "I Can't Handle Distance" Panic

Scenario: You and your best friend have a small disagreement. They say they need a little space, but within minutes, you're sending multiple texts, checking their status, replaying the conversation, and asking, "Are we okay?"

What Dependency Looks Like: Space feels unbearable. You interpret distance as danger, and your nervous system scrambles for closeness, even if it means ignoring your own needs. *"If they need space, something must be terribly wrong. I can't lose them, I need to fix this right now."*

2. The "Why Haven't They Texted Back?" Spiral

Scenario: You text your crush something funny or vulnerable. They leave you on read. You stare at your phone for hours, rereading what you said, wondering if you came off clingy or weird.

What Dependency Looks Like: A delayed reply starts to unravel your self-confidence. Your brain turns one unanswered message into a reflection of your worth. *"They probably think I'm annoying. I always say the wrong thing. Why can't I just be normal and likable for once?"*

3. The "I Don't Know Who I Am Without Them" Trap

Scenario: You and your partner used to do everything together. Study sessions, music playlists, even matching bios. Now that they're distant or things ended, you feel like your days are empty and your identity is unclear.

What Dependency Looks Like: Your sense of self was built around them. Without them, life feels colorless, directionless. *"Everything reminds me of them. I don't even know what shows I actually like or what music I enjoy anymore. Who am I supposed to be now?"*

4. The "If They're Upset, I Must've Messed Up" Reflex

Scenario: A close friend seems distant. They're not texting like usual or sound short over lunch. You immediately assume you did something wrong, and start apologizing or overcompensating, even though they haven't said anything.

What Dependency Looks Like: You take emotional responsibility for other people's moods. You become hyper-aware and self-blaming anytime there's tension. *"They seem off today. I must have said something stupid. I always mess things up without realizing it. I should apologize before they get more upset."*

5. The "I Have to Earn My Place" Cycle

Scenario: You're always the one making plans, sending the "are you okay?" texts first, offering to pay when you hang out, and staying up late to give pep talks, even when you're running on empty. You secretly wonder if they'd show up for you the same way. **What Dependency Looks Like:** Your place in people's lives feels conditional, like if you stop being useful, you'll stop being wanted. *"If I don't check in on them, they might forget about me. I need to be the one they can always count on, or why would they keep me around?"*

6. The "I Can't Let Them Stay Mad at Me" Cycle

Scenario: You have a friend who's often upset with you over something you said, forgot, or didn't do "right." You spend hours trying to fix it, overexplaining, apologizing again and again, even when it wasn't really your fault.

What Dependency Looks Like: You feel responsible for their constant disappointment and start walking on eggshells to avoid triggering them. *"I should have known that would upset them. I'm such an idiot. I'll do whatever it takes to make this right, even if it means taking all the blame."*

7. The "I Shape Myself Around Them" Habit

Scenario: Your friend has strong opinions, cool style, confident energy, and you start picking up all their hobbies, jokes, and even their taste in music or clothes. You find yourself holding back your actual opinions just to match theirs.

What Dependency Looks Like: You shift who you are to stay liked or "good enough" in their eyes, even if it means losing parts of your true personality. *"I can't tell them I actually hate that movie they love. They'd think I have terrible taste. Better to just agree and try to see why everyone thinks it's so great."*

Moving Forward

Healing emotional dependency isn't about becoming distant. It's about learning how to care without losing yourself, how to stay connected and still rooted in who you are. That kind of peace begins inside you, and it's something you can return to, again and again.

Practice: The Relationship Roots Inventory

This practice helps you identify where emotional dependency might be affecting your relationships and guides you through concrete steps to build more inner security. This is about gradually strengthening your emotional foundation so you can love from wholeness, not from need.

The Emotional Dependency Check-In

This is not about blaming yourself or labeling your relationships. It's just a way to gently notice patterns. Be honest, be kind, and remember, this is just for you.

You can do this for one relationship that feels emotionally intense, or try it with a few different ones to spot any patterns.

Part 1: Identifying Your Dependency Patterns

1. Mood Connection

How much does this person's mood, attention, or approval affect mine?▢
Rate it from 1–10
(1 = I feel pretty separate, 10 = My mood really depends on them)*Example: "With my best friend Maya, probably a 7. If she's upset or distant, I get anxious even if it's not about me."*

2. Identity Check

Complete the sentence for this relationship:
"Without this person, I would feel _______."*Example: "Without my boyfriend, I would feel a little lost. Like I wouldn't know who to talk to or what to do on weekends."*

This isn't good or bad. It just shows how connected your sense of identity is to this rel*ationship.*

3. Anxiety Signals

Which of these show up for you in this relationship?

Check any that feel familiar.

☐ Checking your phone a lot waiting for their reply

☐ Apologizing a lot, even for small things

☐ Feeling panic or urgency if they pull away

☐ Struggling to share what you need

☐ Overthinking what you say or how you come across

☐ Worrying you're "too much" or "not enough"

☐ Canceling your own plans to stay available for them

*Example: "With Maya, I definitely overthink my texts.
I'll rewrite them or feel anxious if she doesn't respond fast."*

4. Authenticity Gap

Do you ever catch yourself doing any of these in this relationship?

☐ Holding back your real opinions to keep things smooth

☐ Pretending to be into something they like (when you're not)

☐ Hiding your needs because you don't want to be a burden

☐ Keeping your struggles to yourself to avoid making them uncomfortable*Example:
"I usually don't talk about my family stuff with him because I'm afraid he'll think
I'm being dramatic."*

Reminder:

You're not doing anything wrong by caring deeply about someone.

This check-in just helps you understand where your emotional energy is going, and
whether your sense of self is getting tangled up in the process.

The Self-Anchoring Action Plan

Now that you've identified where emotional dependency might be shaping your relationships, it's time to build your inner foundation. This plan is about making small, steady shifts, so your sense of worth comes from within, not from someone else's reaction or presence.

Step 1: Choose One Relationship to Focus On

Pick one relationship that feels the most emotionally charged or where you notice your sense of self gets shaken.

This could be:
A friendship where you feel like you have to stay "on" all the time
A relationship where you lose confidence when they pull back
A family dynamic where your needs often get silenced

Step 2: Choose One Small Shift to Practice

Choose one realistic, manageable shift to practice in this relationship. You're not trying to overhaul everything. One small move is enough to start changing the pattern.

Examples:
Wait 30 minutes before replying to a non-urgent text (practice space)
Share one real opinion instead of staying silent (practice truth)
Plan one solo activity each week you enjoy (practice independence)
Say, "I'll need to get back to you" instead of instantly saying yes (practice boundaries)

Step 3: Build Your Discomfort Toolkit

Changing patterns feels uncomfortable You're creating new responses, and that takes support. Create a toolkit to ground yourself when the pull to depend feels strongest.

Physical Anchor

A quick body-based practice to bring you back to center:

- Take 5 deep breaths with your hand on your chest

- Press your feet into the ground and feel the floor beneath you

- Splash cold water on your face

- Stretch or shake out your hands and shoulders

Mental Reminder

Choose a phrase that speaks to your deeper truth. Repeat it when anxiety or fear rises:

- "Their mood doesn't define me."

- "I can care without collapsing."

- "It's okay to take up space."

- "My peace starts within."

Redirection Plan

List a few go-to activities that can help shift your attention and reconnect you to yourself:

- Text a different friend

- Go outside and move your body

- Write about what you're feeling

- Draw, create, or listen to music

- Do a task you've been putting off, something that brings you back into action

Real-Life Example: Jordan's Journey

Relationship Focus: Relationship with their dad

Dependency Patterns Jordan Noticed

- Only sharing achievements, never struggles

- Avoiding topics that might lead to disagreement

- Feeling like they always need to be "strong" to avoid disappointing him

- Withholding feelings to keep the peace

Small Shift Chosen

"I will tell my dad one small thing I'm struggling with this week, instead of pretending everything is fine."

This shift helps Jordan practice vulnerability and challenge the idea that they only deserve love when they're doing well.

Jordan's Discomfort Toolkit

Physical Anchor
Slow exhale while pressing palms together, feeling grounded through the hands

Mental Reminder
"I can be loved even when I'm not holding it all together."

Redirection Plan
Journal a few honest thoughts before talking to Dad
Listen to calming music
Go for a short walk to release tension

Progress Snapshot (Week 1)

Date	Dependency Urge	What I Did Instead	How It Felt
Tue	Wanted to say "everything's fine" when he asked about school	Mentioned feeling overwhelmed by deadlines	A little awkward, but relieving
Thu	Avoided bringing up a disagreement	Gently shared their point of view	Nervous, but felt respected
Sat	Felt pressure to smile through dinner	Took a few breaths and just stayed quiet instead of performing	Calm and more present

A Reminder for Jordan—and You

You don't have to earn connection by being impressive.

Honesty creates space for deeper closeness, especially when it feels risky.

Real-Life Example: Alexis' Journey

Relationship Focus: Longtime best friend, Dani

Dependency Patterns Alexis Noticed

- Always being the one to reach out and make plans

- Feeling anxious when Dani doesn't reply right away

- Saying "yes" to hangouts even when feeling tired

- Feeling responsible for Dani's moods

Small Shift Chosen

"I will wait until I genuinely want to hang out before saying yes, instead of responding out of guilt or habit."

This shift helps Alexis build boundaries without disconnecting.

Alexis' Discomfort Toolkit

Physical Anchor

Put hand on heart and inhale for 4 seconds, exhale for 6

Mental Reminder

"Saying no sometimes doesn't make me a bad friend, it makes me an honest one."

Redirection Plan

Read a chapter of a book

Text a different friend just to connect

Take a short nap or journal about the guilt

Progress Snapshot (Week 1)

Date	Dependency Urge	What I Did Instead	How It Felt
Mon	Said "yes" to hang out even though I was exhausted	Texted, "Can we do Friday instead?"	Empowered, a little guilty
Wed	Worried when she didn't respond all day	Left phone in another room and read for 30 mins	Hard at first, then peaceful
Sat	Wanted to joke instead of sharing how I really felt	Told her I was feeling off	Nervous, but she was kind

A Reminder for Alexis—and You

A real friendship doesn't need you to be "on" all the time.

It needs you to be **real**.

When you show up honestly, you give others permission to do the same.

Real-Life Example: Sam's Journey

Relationship Focus: Early relationship with their crush, Jordan

Dependency Patterns Sam Noticed

- Overanalyzing every text and rereading conversations

- Avoiding sharing real opinions to seem more likable

- Constantly asking friends, "What do you think they meant by this?" Feeling anxious when Jordan takes a while to reply

Small Shift Chosen

"I will express one small, honest opinion this week instead of always agreeing with what Jordan says."

This shift helps Sam build confidence in showing up as themselves, not a curated version they hope Jordan will like.

Sam's Discomfort Toolkit

Physical Anchor
Touching fingertips together while taking 5 slow breaths

Mental Reminder
"I'm not here to perform. I'm here to connect."

Redirection Plan
Work on art
Call a friend to talk about something unrelated
Go outside and move their body

Progress Snapshot (Week 1)

Date	Dependency Urge	What I Did Instead	How It Felt
Tue	Almost said I liked a show I've never seen	Said "I actually haven't watched it but I'm curious now"	Scary for a second, then real
Thu	Wanted to double-text when he didn't reply	Put my phone down and painted for 20 minutes	Less panicked than usual
Sun	Felt nervous to admit I was feeling off	Sent a text saying "Hey, I'm feeling a little low today. Just being honest."	Vulnerable, but proud

A Reminder for Sam—and You

Being liked for a version of you that isn't real doesn't lead to real closeness.

The more you bring your true self into the room, the more you find out who really sees you, and who's just drawn to the performance.

You are already interesting, lovable, and enough as you are.

3. Relational Compassion: Seeing Beyond the Surface

From Self-Protection to Compassionate Connection

Now that you've begun to loosen emotional dependency and build a stronger sense of self, your relationships can shift too. When you stop needing people to validate or complete you, you start seeing them more clearly.

Instead of focusing on what someone gives you, or how they make you feel, you begin to notice who they are. You see their emotions, patterns, and humanity. And that's where compassion begins.

Compassion doesn't mean becoming a doormat or excusing hurtful behavior. It means relating from clarity, not just reactivity. It's emotional strength, not softness. And it can transform how you move through friendships, conflict, group dynamics, and everyday interactions.

From Judgment to Understanding

Compassion can sound vague, like something only extra patient or constantly chill people do.

But really, it's just this:
The willingness to pause before assuming.
To ask, "What else might be going on here?"

Judgment is quick. It's easy. Especially in high school, online, or anywhere people are performing versions of themselves.

You might catch yourself thinking:

- "Ugh, she's such a pick-me."

- "He's so full of himself."

- "They're only doing that for attention."

But pause for a moment.

That "pick-me" energy? Might come from never feeling chosen.
That confidence? Might be covering up fear of not being enough.
That loudness? Might be a way to feel seen in the only way they know how.

You don't need to know everyone's story to soften your view.
You just need the curiosity to remember there *is* a story.

Compassion doesn't mean staying in unhealthy situations.
It just means you stop writing people off without looking deeper.
And the more secure you become in yourself, the easier that becomes.

The Backstory Mindset: Practicing Compassion in Real Time

Instead of jumping to conclusions, try asking:

"What might be going on underneath this behavior?"

Not to excuse it, but to understand it.

Here are five common relationship moments where that shift in mindset can provide an opportunity for compassion.

The Loud Kid in Class

You're trying to focus, and they keep cracking jokes or interrupting. The first thought might be, *"They're just annoying."*

But zoom out: maybe they use humor to mask anxiety. Maybe being loud is how they avoid feeling invisible.

Compassion means you can still feel frustrated and also recognize they might be struggling.

The Friend Who Ghosts You

They stop texting, cancel plans, and feel distant. You might assume, *"They don't care anymore."*

But maybe they're overwhelmed, anxious, or going through something they haven't shared.

Instead of spiraling into self-doubt, compassion helps you stay grounded in your own center.

The Online Oversharer

They post every breakdown on social media, and it's tempting to roll your eyes.

But compassion wonders: *"Maybe this is how they ask for help. Maybe they don't have anyone to talk to."*

You don't have to engage, but the way you *feel* changes when you see the human behind the post.

The Parent Who's Always Nagging

You feel like you can't breathe without a question about homework or a comment on your choices.

It's exhausting. But compassion asks: *"Could this be their way of worrying?"*

Understanding doesn't mean you agree, but it can soften how much it gets under your skin.

The Mean Girl (or Guy) at School

They gossip. They exclude people. Their compliments come with a sting.

Compassion wonders: *"What kind of pain makes tearing others down feel like power?"*

This doesn't mean letting them off the hook, but it keeps *you* from taking their behavior personally.

Why Compassion Matters in Relationships

Less Stress for You

Judging others might feel satisfying for a second, but it builds tension—like carrying around a mental glare. Compassion clears that weight. It's not about agreeing; it's about finding peace.

More Real Connection

People feel when you're trying to understand them instead of judging them. That's what opens the door to honest conversations, fewer misunderstandings, and more space to just be human together.

Stronger Boundaries

Compassion doesn't mean letting things slide. In fact, the clearer you are about someone's patterns, the easier it becomes to respond with calm, steady boundaries—without guilt.

Compassion ≠ Forgiveness (Unless You Want It To)

Let's be clear: compassion is not the same as forgiveness.

It doesn't mean what they did was okay.
It means: **"I'm choosing not to carry this judgment anymore."**

That's emotional maturity.
You can still walk away, still block them, still speak your truth.
But from a place of self-respect, not bitterness.

Quick Practice: The 60-Second Relationship Reset

What it's for: When someone frustrates you and you're about to spiral, shut down, or snap back.

Step 1: Name what you're feeling.

Say it to yourself honestly:
"I feel left out."
"I feel judged."
"I feel hurt."

Naming the feeling helps you step out of the swirl and into awareness.

Step 2: Flip the lens.

Ask yourself:
"What might they be feeling right now?"

You don't have to know for sure. Just wonder:
"Maybe they're anxious."
"Maybe they're overwhelmed."
"Maybe they're stuck in their own stuff."

Then ask:
"Can I protect my peace and still recognize that theirs might be missing?"

This isn't about excusing the behavior. It's about seeing clearly—without carrying what isn't yours.

Step 3: Choose your next move.

Pick one grounded response that honors both your truth and your calm:
—Send a calm or neutral reply
—Take space instead of reacting
—Name your truth gently
—Say nothing and let the moment pass

You're not here to fix them. You're here to stay rooted in yourself.

Final Thought

Compassion isn't weakness. It's presence.

It's choosing clarity when your ego wants chaos.

It's taking one honest breath when everything inside wants to scream.

You don't need to save the whole relationship.

But with just 60 seconds of compassion, you might save your peace.

Chapter 5 Wrap-Up: Redefining Self in Relationships

Here's what you explored:

Relationship Patterns and the Prism of Identity

You saw how your identity bends through different relationships, like light through a prism. Many of these shifts began as strengths: adaptability, caretaking, peacemaking. But when they come from fear or habit rather than choice, you can lose connection with your full self. This is the Relationship Identity Trap.

Reclaiming Authenticity

You learned to recognize the invisible agreements shaping who you're "allowed" to be, and how to gently rewrite them. Being authentic doesn't mean being the same everywhere. It means choosing how you show up, staying anchored in your truth, and letting your light stay visible even as it shifts.

Moving Beyond Emotional Dependency

You uncovered how dependency shows up in subtle ways, when your mood, confidence, or sense of self becomes tied to someone else's presence or approval. Through reflection and small, grounding shifts, you began building a deeper inner foundation, so your connections can be rooted in wholeness, not need.

Practicing Relational Compassion

You practiced seeing beyond surface behaviors, recognizing that everyone is carrying something, just like you. Compassion isn't about excusing. It's about responding with clarity instead of reactivity. You learned how to protect your peace while still honoring someone else's humanity.

And most importantly, you remembered this:

You don't have to perform to stay loved.
You don't have to overgive to be included.
You don't have to shrink to feel safe.

You are allowed to take up space.

You are allowed to change and be seen.

You are allowed to stay rooted in your truth, even while staying connected to others.

Next Up: Chapter 6 — Finding Your Center

You've learned to witness your thoughts, feel your emotions, return to presence, rediscover purpose, and show up more fully in relationships.

Now, it's time to turn inward again, not to escape, but to reconnect with something even deeper:

Your inner guidance

Your quiet wisdom

Your steady peace

Your natural creativity and spiritual presence

In Chapter 6, you'll learn how to tap into the part of you that stays calm even when life gets loud. The part that already knows what matters.

Quote: "Be yourself. No one can ever tell you you're doing it wrong." Matt Haig
Song: "Grow As We Go" Ben Platt

Chapter Six

Unlocking the Invisible

Introduction: The Hidden Dimension

This chapter might feel a little out there. Some of it may even sound cheesy at first. That's okay.

You don't have to believe anything or force yourself to feel a certain way.

This is just about noticing a part of you that doesn't always get airtime. The quiet awareness beneath the stress, the sense of calm that shows up when you stop performing, the moments when life feels bigger than just what's happening on the surface.

Maybe you've felt it during a walk, a late-night drive, a song that hits deep, or a conversation that left you feeling more alive.

That space isn't imaginary. It's real. And it's yours.

This chapter is about learning how to return to it. To feel more grounded, more connected, and more fully yourself.

1. The Quiet Center: Your Inner Sanctuary

Discovering the One Who's Aware

In Chapter 1, we explored how you can step back and notice your thoughts. You can watch them come and go, like stars in the sky. This helps you feel less overwhelmed. But now let's go a little deeper.

Remember, If you can notice your thoughts... who is doing the noticing?

That quiet part of you, the one that sees your thoughts, your feelings, and what's happening around you, is what we call awareness.

Awareness is not the same as your thoughts. It's not your emotions. It's not your personality. It is the part of you that is always paying attention. Even when your thoughts are spinning, even when you feel upset or confused, awareness is still there in the background, watching it all happen.

Awareness doesn't argue or react. It just sees. And that's what makes it powerful.

You've probably felt it before. Those quick moments when you suddenly realize you're observing your own experience:

- When you're walking home listening to music and notice, *"I actually feel really at peace right now."*

- When you're laughing with friends and catch yourself thinking, *"This is one of those memories I'll hold onto."*

- When you're working on a creative project and realize, *"I'm so focused right now. It's like time disappeared."*

- When you're watching the sunset or looking at the stars and feel yourself quietly thinking, *"Whoa. I'm really here."*

- When you're studying or practicing and notice, *"I'm actually learning this. I'm in it."*

That feeling of presence, that quiet, grounded awareness, is already inside you. You're not doing anything extra. You're just fully here. And that's where your quiet center lives.

Your Inner World Creates Your Experience

Everything you experience, what you see, hear, feel, or think, takes shape inside your awareness. The world exists outside of you, yet your experience of it is entirely internal. Light enters your eyes, sound reaches your ears, and your brain turns those signals into meaning. Your awareness receives all of it. This is how you live your life, from the inside.

There's a strange truth in that: you are both a small part of the universe, and the center of everything you know. You are one person among billions, and yet the world you live in only exists as you experience it. You don't control the outside world, but the way it feels to you depends on how it moves through your awareness.

This doesn't mean the world is imagined. It means your experience is personal. Everything comes to life within your awareness like your thoughts, your emotions, your beliefs, your attention. They shape the world you live in, moment by moment.

And at the center of it all is the part of you that sees. The part that notices your thoughts without being swept away. The part that hears your inner voice and doesn't rush to argue. The one who watches it all with clarity, even if just for a second.

This is not a contradiction. It's a kind of balance. You are in the world, and the world is also inside you. When you remember that, something opens. You begin to see that your life is not just something happening to you. It's something rising from within you.

Practice: Noticing the One Who Notices (1 Minute)

This simple practice helps you connect with your awareness. You can do it anytime, anywhere.

1. **Sit quietly** for a moment. Let your body settle.

2. **Feel your body.** Notice your feet on the floor. Notice your breathing. Notice the temperature of the air.

3. **Watch your thoughts.** Just observe them. Don't try to stop them. Let them come and go.

4. **Now ask yourself:** "Who is noticing all of this?"

5. **Rest there.** Even if just for a few seconds. Just stay with that quiet awareness that's watching everything.

This is not about escaping reality. It's about experiencing it from a deeper place. From your quiet center, you gain perspective, clarity, and a sense of spaciousness that transforms how you move through the day.

You can return to this place whenever you need it. It's always here. It's always you.

2. Your Energy Field: The Vibrance of Being

The Living Current

There is something alive moving through you all the time. It powers your heartbeat, your breath, your thoughts, and your presence. Some people call it energy. You don't have to name it to feel it.

Science shows that your body gives off a real electromagnetic field, especially around your heart and brain. Artists often show this by drawing light around a person. Athletes feel it when they're "in the zone." You are not just your muscles and bones. You are movement, feeling, and presence.

You can sense this energy directly.

Try This: The Hand Energy Experiment

1. Rub your hands together for about 10 to 15 seconds until they feel warm.

2. Slowly separate them so there's about an inch of space between your palms.

3. Focus on the space between your hands. See if you notice any tingling, warmth, or a gentle push-pull sensation.

4. Move your hands slightly closer, then further apart. Pay attention to how that feels.

5. Close your eyes and bring your attention to the rest of your body. Can you feel this same kind of energy around your chest, your arms, your whole body?

This is your energy field. It's real. And the more you notice it, the more alive and connected you feel.

Energy Awareness in Daily Life

Once you become aware of this energy, you'll start to notice it in all kinds of moments:

During Creative Activities:

- Feel the energy moving through your hands as you draw, write, or build

- Notice how your whole body gets involved when you're fully into what you're doing

- Let ideas and inspiration flow through you instead of forcing them

In Nature and Open Spaces:

- Notice how your body feels when you're around trees, plants, or the ocean

- Feel yourself open up when you're in wide, quiet places

- Sense the connection between your body and the space around you

In Social Connections:

- Pay attention to how it feels when someone you care about is near, even without speaking

- Notice how the energy between you and others can feel light, heavy, warm, or distant

- Sense how being real and open with someone creates a kind of shared field between you

This awareness helps you feel more connected, not just to yourself, but to the people and spaces around you. You don't have to make anything happen. You just notice what's already there.

3. Flow State: Tapping the Creative Current

As you've started exploring your awareness and energy, you've probably noticed there are moments when everything just clicks. You're not overthinking. You're not trying too hard. You're just in it. That feeling? That's called **flow**.

Athletes call it being "in the zone." Musicians call it "finding the groove." Psychologists call it **flow state**. But whatever you call it, you've probably felt it before.

In a flow state:

- **Time feels like it slows down** or disappears
  Example: You're gaming, drawing, or writing and realize hours have passed, but it only felt like minutes.

- **You stop being self-conscious**
  Example: You're dancing or singing with your friends, not thinking about how you look or sound. Just enjoying it.

- **You and the activity feel like one thing**
  Example: You're skating, coding, or practicing a sport, and it feels like your body and focus are totally in sync.

- **It feels smooth, natural, and focused**
  Example: You're playing an instrument or building something with your hands, and everything clicks.

- **You feel completely alive in the moment**
  Example: You're laughing with someone you trust, and nothing else is in your head.

Flow feels amazing, but there's something even deeper happening underneath it. Sometimes, in the quiet space that flow creates, something new starts to rise. A sentence. An image. A solution. A gut feeling about what needs to happen next.

That's **inspiration**.

Where Inspiration Comes From

Inspiration is not something you control or force, it's something you **catch**. Like a radio signal you weren't even trying to tune into.

You might feel it when:

- You're painting and suddenly know what to add

- You're walking and a new idea just hits

- You're journaling and a deeper truth comes out on the page

- You're helping a friend and know exactly what to say

This is what some artists, writers, and creators call the **creative source**. They say ideas "come through them," like they didn't invent them. They just made space for them to land.

That source isn't separate from you. It's a deeper layer of you. Beneath the noise and pressure of everyday thoughts.

Flow + Inspiration = Creative Magic

Flow is the ride.
Inspiration is the wave.
Together, they make up the creative current.

When you learn how to **relax, focus, and open up**, this current becomes more accessible.

That's where your most real, surprising, and meaningful creativity lives.

The Flow + Inspiration Practice

For when you want to get in the zone, make something cool, or just stop spiraling for a sec.

This isn't about being a "creative genius." It's about giving your brain some room to breathe and your ideas a chance to show up.

1. Pick your vibe

Choose something that pulls you in. Could be:

- Drawing, building, writing, dancing, designing a playlist

- Or just messing around with something a little challenging but fun
  If it's boring, you'll zone out. If it's too hard, you'll doom scroll. Find your sweet spot.

2. Clear the chaos

Shut the tabs. Mute the texts. Put your phone face down like it betrayed you. Give yourself a tiny window to *just be here.*

3. Set the vibe, not the pressure

Tell yourself:

"I don't need to make something amazing. I'm just here to see what shows up."

No goals. No grades. Just curiosity.

4. Just start already

Don't wait for the perfect idea. Open the sketchbook. Hit record. Doodle something weird.
Flow doesn't come when you wait. It shows up once you're moving.

5. Chase what feels good-weird

If something sparks even the *tiniest* spark—follow it.
Could be a color, a word, a line, a sound. Doesn't have to make sense. Trust the little
"ooh."

6. Ignore the peanut gallery

That voice in your head going: "This sucks"?
Cool. Thank it for its opinion. Then keep going anyway.
Every creative person you admire? They ignore that voice too.

7. Pause + notice

When you're done, stop for a sec.
Look at what came through. Maybe it's messy. Maybe it's cool.
Either way, it came from *you*.

That's the part that matters.

Why This Matters

Flow and inspiration remind you that you're more than your to-do list, your grades,
or your social media feed.
You're creative. You're connected. You have something inside you that knows what
to do. If you make space to listen.

You don't have to force creativity.
You **tap into it.**

And when you do, you remember something important:
Your ideas matter.
Your energy matters.
You matter.

4. Awe: Touching the Vast

From Flow to Wonder

In the last section, we explored flow, the state where you become so fully immersed in something that your sense of self disappears for a while.

Now we're going even further into that feeling of expansion. This next part isn't about doing anything at all. It's about being open to something bigger showing up around you, something that makes you stop and go: *Whoa*.

The Perspective-Shifting Power of Wonder

Awe is that breath-catching feeling when you encounter something so beautiful, huge, or mysterious that it completely shifts your view of the world. It can show up in a quiet moment or hit you out of nowhere. It's that spark of wonder that makes everything feel more alive.

You've probably felt it:

- Standing under a sky full of stars

- Watching lightning flash across the clouds

- Hearing a song that makes your chest feel full

- Seeing someone do something insanely kind or talented

This feeling isn't just cool, it's powerful. Studies show that awe:

- Expands your sense of time

- Takes focus off your problems

- Increases your connection to the world around you

- Helps you feel like part of something bigger

- Opens your mind and your heart

Awe softens the tight grip of your everyday identity and connects you to something deeper. It's another way to experience that infinite part of you.

Sources of Awe: Where Wonder Lives

You don't need a mountaintop or a spaceship to feel awe. You just need to *notice* with full attention. Here are some reliable places to look:

Digital Awe Sources

- NASA or space photos that zoom way out

- 4K nature videos that show wild landscapes

- Art that makes your brain light up

- Music that gives you chills

- Videos of people doing the impossible

- Science facts that make you rethink reality

IRL Awe Sources

- Looking up at the sky, especially at sunrise, sunset, or at night

- Standing near a body of water—even a small one

- Watching plants grow in unexpected places

- Seeing someone do something with complete mastery

- A stranger showing unexpected kindness

- Hearing a live song that moves you to silence

Awe doesn't depend on the size of what you're looking at. It depends on your ability to see it with wonder.

The Awe Practice: Cultivating Regular Wonder

You can actually train yourself to feel awe more often. Here's how:

1. **Choose an awe source.** Pick something you already know gives you that "wow" feeling—music, nature, art, science, whatever works for you.

2. **Make space.** Give yourself a few uninterrupted minutes. No multitasking.

3. **Open your senses.** Don't just look. *See.* Don't just listen. *Hear.* Let yourself slow down enough to really take it in.

4. **Let it move you.** Don't rush the moment. If you feel goosebumps, stillness, or even tears, that's part of it.

5. **Notice the shift.** Afterward, reflect: How did that change your mood? Your thoughts? Your sense of being?

Every time you pause to take in something vast, something beautiful, something unexpected, you're practicing expansion. You're reconnecting with the part of you that already knows there's more to life than just getting through the day.

But wonder doesn't only arrive in the grand and extraordinary. It's not limited to sunsets or starry skies. Sometimes, the most powerful moments are the ones that seem small, the ones we usually rush past.

Because awe isn't just out there. It's also right here.

5. Everyday Presence: The Infinite in the Ordinary

Real-Life Moments That Actually Matter

Earlier, you explored how stillness, energy, creativity, and awe can help you feel more connected. Now it's time to bring that same kind of presence into your everyday life, the parts that seem small or boring or not worth noticing.

The truth is, you don't need a big, deep moment to feel connected to something real. You just need to pay attention to what's already here. The ordinary stuff can feel surprisingly alive when you slow down enough to actually experience it.

It's not about adding more to your life. It's about noticing what's already in it.

The Power of Attention

When you bring real attention to something, it changes how you experience it. It doesn't change the moment—it changes you.

It's like switching on a filter where everything sharpens. You start seeing textures, patterns, and weird little details you normally miss.

That's the kind of attention we're practicing here.

The Everyday Presence Practice

Try this whenever you want to feel more grounded or connected to the moment you're in.

1. **Pick something normal.** Brushing your teeth, tying your shoes, pouring a drink, walking somewhere, listening to music.

2. **Slow it down.** Do it just a little slower than usual. It makes everything feel more real.

3. **Use your senses.** Notice the colors, the sounds, the textures. Feel your body move.

4. **Drop the inner commentary.** Stop explaining it to yourself. Just be in it.

5. **Notice the space.** Tune into the part of you that's watching it all happen.

6. **Let a little awe sneak in.** It's wild that this moment even exists. Let that land.

Some sample lines to get you going (cheese warning):

Brushing Your Teeth

"My brain is making my arm move so I can scrub the bones that live in my face. That's teamwork."

Tying Your Shoes

"Somehow this loop is the way I tie my shoes. And I've just accepted that."

Walking to Class

"Each step is a coordinated muscle miracle. My legs are just casually carrying me like it's no big deal."

Washing Your Hands

"I'm slathering bubble juice on my skin to fight invisible germs. Drama and science in one."

Checking Your Phone

"This glowing brick beams images from space and texts from my friends. And I use it to watch cat videos."

Listening to Someone Talk

"Their vocal cords are vibrating and my ears are turning that into meaning. Language is basically telepathy."

Looking at Water

"This liquid is just a bunch of molecules holding hands. And yet it hydrates my entire existence."

When you start looking at life with this kind of awareness, the small stuff feels different. Not because anything changed, but because you did.

Presence isn't far away. It's in your next breath. It's in your next blink. It's in whatever comes after this sentence.

Chapter 6 Wrap-Up: Living from the Infinite

In this chapter, you explored the deeper parts of yourself. Here's what you connected with:

The Quiet Center

The part of you that can notice everything happening without getting pulled into it.

It reminds you that peace is already inside you.

Your Energy Field

The living current that moves through you and around you.

It reminds you that you are always connected.

Flow State

That feeling when you're fully in it and everything else fades.

It reminds you that you're focused, alive, and fully here.

Awe

The feeling that takes your breath away when something vast or beautiful opens your eyes.

It reminds you that there is more to life than what you can explain.

Everyday Magic

The moments that seem small but feel full when you slow down.

It reminds you that the infinite is always near.

These aren't separate ideas. They're different ways of touching the same truth:
You are not separate from life.
You are part of it.
And the more you notice that, the more alive you feel.

Quote: "May you experience each day as a sacred gift woven around the heart of wonder." John O'Donohue
Song: "Holoscene" Bon Iver

Outro

Journey into Joyful Authenticity

What a journey this has been.

When we began, maybe you felt uncertain. Maybe you were stuck in your head, carrying pressure, self-doubt, or the chaos of growing up. Like so many young people, you were moving through the storm of becoming, quietly asking the big questions:

Who am I, really?
What matters to me?
How do I find my place in all of this?

Chapter by chapter, you kept showing up. You met each idea with honesty, with curiosity, and with a willingness to look inward.

In Chapter 1, you stepped back from your thoughts. You noticed the stories in your mind and realized they do not define you.

In Chapter 2, you met your emotional pain with compassion. You saw it not as a flaw, but as a doorway to healing.

In Chapter 3, you practiced presence. You returned to your life with openness and a sense of calm.

In Chapter 4, you explored purpose. You discovered that it begins to rise when you learn to live from the inside.

In Chapter 5, you carried that truth into your relationships. You started releasing the old roles that no longer fit. You made room for more of your real self to come through.

In Chapter 6, you reached into something deeper. You felt the stillness beneath your thoughts. You caught glimpses of wonder in everyday moments. You experienced a steady sense of connection that lives within you and around you.

This book was never here to fix you. It was here to remind you of what has always been true. Everything you need is already inside you.

Now, you are moving through the world in a new way. You are listening inward. You are speaking from the heart. You are learning to pause. To breathe. To feel a sense of home within yourself.

There is no finish line. You will keep learning. Life will keep changing. But now you carry something steady with you.

You have tools to return to your center.
You have practices that help you stay grounded.
You have a deeper trust in your voice, your rhythm, and your way.

You are not broken.
You are not behind.

You are whole.
You are powerful.
You are deeply, wildly needed.

So keep showing up. Bring your weirdness. Bring your softness. Bring your fire. Be curious. Be kind. Be real. Let yourself be seen. Not only by others—but by yourself.

And when life feels messy or unclear, remember this:

You are already enough.
Not someday.
Not after you figure everything out.
Now. Just as you are.

Thank you for walking this path. I see you. I believe in you. And I am grateful you made it here.

Quote: "You do not become yourself. You return to yourself." Brianna West
Song: "Sleeping At Last" Saturn